Berry Pomeroy Castle

By
Deryck Seymour

With Illustrations by
Jack Hazzard

Berry Pomeroy has belonged to the Seymour family for over four centuries. It is therefore with pleasure that this book is inscribed to Percy Hamilton Seymour, eighteenth Duke of Somerset.

The drawings in this book are dedicated to the memory of the late Mr. W. G. Bennett, Parish Councillor and Chairman for many years.

*First published in 1982
by Deryck Seymour
Arlesey Dene, Mill Lane, Torquay, Devon
Typeset and printed in Great Britain by
Penwell Ltd., Parkwood, Callington,
Cornwall.*

*© Deryck Seymour 1982
ISBN
0 9505949 1 1*

CONTENTS

Acknowledgements	iv
Bibliography	v
Introduction	7
1. The castle Buildings	11
2. Berry under the Pomeroys	43
3. Berry under the Seymours	65
4. The Folklore	85
5. The Hauntings	109
6. The Deer Parks	121
7. Documents and Letters	127
8. Early references, books and letters	133
9. The Parish Church of St Mary	145
10. Botany	159
11. Index of persons and places	163
12. Index of subjects	166

ACKNOWLEDGEMENTS

The production of a book, however small, takes time and trouble. It cannot as a rule be achieved alone, for the author in his researches is bound to seek the help and guidance of those who have just that particular piece of information to impart which he requires at the moment of writing. To all such who have helped me I extend my thanks, hoping that among the names below I have not omitted any.

First of all I must thank Jack Hazzard, my expert collaborator, without whose delightful drawings this book would have been a dull affair. And together with him goes Mrs. Hazzard who provided so many cups of tea and good things to eat whenever we got together to discuss and plan the book. Then next I must thank the staff of the Wiltshire County Record Office at Trowbridge and particularly Miss Lambert; also Mrs. Rowe and the staff of the Devon County Record Office at Exeter; Mr. Dowdell and the staff at the Torquay Public Library Reference Department, and the Public Record Office in Chancery Lane; the Society of Psychical Research; Laurence Garner and the Dry Stone Walling Association.

Among others who have helped are His Grace the Duke of Somerset, the Rev. R. H. Baker, vicar of Berry Pomeroy, the Rev. J. G. M. Scott, Dr. C. A. Ralegh Radford, F.S.A., the Abbot of Buckfast, Major P. Holden, Mr. A. J. Mills (Bourton), Mr. T. G. Moule (Afton), Mr. J. Parry, Mr. R. Treseder, Colonel W. Seymour, Mr. Peter Underwood, Mr. H. J. Widdicombe (Weston), Mrs. Rowden, Miss E. Beveridge, M.A. If I have inadvertently omitted any other names I do sincerely apologise. Last but not least I must thank Mrs. E. Jerrard who so kindly undertook the listing of the wildflowers growing at or near the castle.

Deryck Seymour,
Arlesey Dene,
Mill Lane,
Torquay

May, 1982

BIBLIOGRAPHY

Bray, Mrs.; "Henry de Pomeroy", 1841, Chapman and Hall.
Combes, Luke M.; "Berry Pomeroy"—A poem in two vols. Printed by Cockrem, 10 Strand, Torquay, 1872.
Cuming, Mrs.; A poem—title unknown. A part printed in Mortimer's "Berry Pomeroy Castle", 19th century.
Dugdale, W.; "The New British Traveller" (Devonshire). 1819.
Leland, John; "Itinerary", 1534-43.
Lysons, Daniel; "Magna Britannia" vol.6, 1822.
Maton, Dr. W. G.; "Observations of the Western Counties of England", 1704-06.
Montague, Edward; "The Castle of Berry Pomeroy". "Totnes Times" and "Western Guardian". 2nd edition, 1892.
Mortimer, T. C. & A. E.; "Berry Pomeroy Castle: An Historical and Descriptive Sketch". Mortimer Bros., Totnes. Early 20th century?
Pole, Sir William; "Collections towards a Description of the County of Devon", ante 1635.
Polwhele, Richard; "History of Devonshire", 1793-1806.
Powley, Edward B.; "The House of de la Pomerai"; Raynor, Sutton and Sons, Liverpool, 1947.
Powley, Edward B.; "Berry Pomeroy Castle". Illustrated Official Guide; Raynor, Sutton and Sons, Liverpool, 1947.
Prince, John; "Worthies of Devon", 1702.
Risdon, Tristram: "Chorographical Description or Survey of the County of Devon", 1630.
St. Maur, H.; "Annals of the Seymours"; Kegan Paul, Trench, Trubner & Co., London, 1902.
Seymour, Deryck; "Torre Abbey", Townsend & Son, 1977.
"Transactions of the Devonshire Association", various volumes.
Westcote, Thomas; "A View of Devonshire" 1630, pub. 1845.
Wishaw, Fred; "A Secret of Berry Pomeroy", Griffith, Farrar, Brown & Co., 1902.
Wood, Mrs. Henry; "Pomeroy Abbey", Richard Bentley & Son, 1878.

Recent Pamphlets
"An Illustrated Guide to Berry Pomeroy Castle, Totnes, Devon",   by A. Clamp.
"Ghost Stories and Legends" by S. M. Ellis.

Further Books by Deryck Seymour
"Torre Abbey" (Townsend, Exeter, 1977) £10.
"Upton—the Heart of Torquay" (Townsend, Exeter, 1963) £1.50.
Obtainable from the author at Arlesey Dene, Mill Lane, Torquay.

Abbreviations
T.D.A—Transactions of the Devonshire Association.
Annals—"Annals of the Seymours".
d.—died
c.—circa

Pen and ink drawing by Willoughby Rooke of the Gatehouse at Berry Pomeroy Castle in 1875

Introduction

For as long as I can remember the castle of Berry Pomeroy has exerted a strange influence over me. Having once visited it as a small boy it has always been at the back of my mind, and I have never at any time forgotten the appearance of those rugged, ivy-clad walls. This constant remembrance has continued through life, whether at home or abroad. I suppose you might almost say that I was haunted by the place, but in a pleasant way. The castle has always seemed to me an unsolved riddle. What did it look like in its hey-day? What went on there? Why was it ever built at all just there? If I were to go there now at this moment, how would it appear? Brooding, gaunt and aloof as usual, I suppose, but what a story those walls could tell! The castle has in a way always issued a kind of challenge to me, and also to my colleague, Jack Hazzard. What could I do for it? I could not rebuild it or recapture the past, but I could write about it; and so this book is an attempt to bring under one cover a consideration of the many aspects from which the castle can be considered. First and foremost comes the venerable group of buildings of which it is composed. These I have tried to assess with regard to their age and former use. Thence it was an easy step to continue by considering the activities of the Pomeroy and Seymour families who between them have owned the castle and manor for over 900 years. Then there had to be an appraisal of the rich vein of folklore which seems to cling to this romantic ruin with a strange persistence. Hand in hand with this fascinating subject goes a yet more dramatic one—the study of those strange occult happenings at Berry which can be traced back for at least two centuries.

All this is more than can be included in a mere guide book—however good. I felt therefore that the time was perhaps ripe for something a little more elaborate, yet still within the bounds of a small book. The result, I hope, may be acceptable to the many who have known and loved the old castle throughout their lives, and also to the host of casual visitors who come there each day.

My hardest task has been to present a logical account of the different periods of building which the ruins display, for there is only the scantiest documentary evidence to help the historian on his lonely way. For instance it is quite amazing to learn that the first written mention of the castle is as late as 1467. Its beginnings are highly problematical and buried in the mists of time. Many may raise an eyebrow at the late date of building which my deductions lead me to suppose—yet they seem to be corroborated by the evidence of recent excavation. Then again some may be disappointed at my conclusion that this was never a place of any strategical strength, for the folklore suggests quite the opposite. The fact has to be admitted that all who have written about the ruins so far have been unable to see the very walls which they were writing about, for they were smothered in a mantle of thick ivy. Now all this has been happily removed, and it is possible to study the walls as never before and learn what they have to tell.

I have written a thumbnail sketch of the lives of all those who in their turn have owned Berry Pomeroy. There were 19 generations of Pomeroys and 18 of Seymours to the present day. But with the latter family I cut my story short with the death of the 4th baronet in 1688, for after that the castle was abandoned to its fate and ceased to be the seat of an illustrious family. The present owner is Percy Hamilton Seymour, the 18th Duke of Somerset, and the castle is looked after by the Ministry of the Environment under Deed of Guardianship (1977).

I trust that the mind of the reader will not suffer too much of a jolt as he switches from fact to fancy, and goes on to read of the folklore and hauntings. Whimsical and fantastic though these stories may be, they are very much a part of the grey and sombre atmosphere which pervades the ruins on even the brightest of summer days.

On the literary side the poems and novels which the legends of

Berry Pomeroy evoked in the 19th century are all considered, for the simple reason that they help us to understand how the castle appeared to the visitor of a century and more ago. The accounts of it written by the county's historians are also considered.

The story of the two deer parks I thought also worthy of inclusion here, because the older, enclosed in 1207, must have preceded the present castle. It consisted of 100 acres then, but the later park is over 340 acres in extent and still encloses the castle and its approaches behind a barrier of some 2.7 miles of most impressive free stone walling. Lastly, space has been found to mention each species of the host of wildflowers which bedeck the broken walls and their surroundings, adding colour and charm to this beautiful place in spring and early summer. A list of the various species will interest botanists.

Exciting things are now happening at Berry, for after years of tranquillity we have seen work on the fabric begin during the last few years. The unusual sight of scaffolding and a team of workmen hard at it are a delight to all who love the castle. Then again the last three summers have seen keen archaeologists, with Miss D. Griffiths at their head, working in the courtyard and kitchen. How rewarding these digs have been, for the splendid colonnade so aptly described by the Rev. John Prince has reappeared, quite transforming the whole aspect of the courtyard. One can but hope that this work will continue and enable us at last to produce a correct plan of the vanished buildings.* As if this were not enough a most unlikely find has been a 15th century fresco on the wall of the guardroom. So at the moment there is an air of expectancy at the castle. What will they find next?

There are, however, certain riddles with regard to the building which are still outstanding, and which are of great importance. Where, for instance, did the castle derive its water supply? Not a single well has been as yet discovered inside the buildings or without. It is quite unthinkable that all water was carried up from the valley below, for the castle could never have survived a siege even of the shortest duration. Then again, if the moat was a wet one, the source of the water which supplied it is problematical owing to the geographical characteristics of the surrounding land. Lastly,

---

*At the moment of writing only an interim plan can be produced for the purposes of this book.

not one garde-robe can be identified with certainty anywhere. This again is absurd, for in a house such as this, which was almost palatial, such a need must have been more than adequately met. So at present we know nothing of the water supply or drainage. Neither do we know anything about the truth or otherwise which concerns those persistent stories of underground vaults and passages. There are still many secrets which those old walls contain. They will only be resolved by determined excavation.

CHAPTER 1

The Castle Buildings

One of the best known ruins in the south-west of England is the castle of Berry Pomeroy, which stands about two and a half miles north-east of the old-world town of Totnes. In its derelict state it has endeared itself to many, and each year it is visited by an increasing number of visitors. Some like to enjoy the great beauty of the surroundings and have a quiet picnic on the lawn before the gatehouse. Children love to clamber up and down the old rampart walls and look for dungeons. To others this castle is sinister, but they go there just the same, half hoping to see something fantastic. All will agree that the place has a fascination all its own, for it seems to draw people like a magnet from the four corners of the earth. One's first visit is always the best remembered, and the sudden appearance of a castle where a moment ago all was thick woodland is never to be forgotten.

The castle stands on a rocky limestone crag and occupies .651 of an acre. It is about 250 feet above sea level and beneath it is the steep-sided valley of the Gatcombe Brook which flows into the little River Hems, itself a tributary of the Dart. The crag forms a spur projecting from a line of 400 foot hills which curve round it in the shape of a crescent. The quite remarkable amphitheatre in which the castle stands is not easy to appreciate, for it is quite invisible in summer on account of the thick woods which clothe the steep slopes of the hills. The woods, if there in bygone ages, could have been used to form a natural defence from the south. The only way then of approaching the castle would have been by the steep climb from the valley. There is still at the foot of the crag, quite a large mill pond which suggests that the active Gatcombe Brook, which never dries up in times of drought, could have been used to flood the whole valley in time of attack. Thus the natural attributes of the site could have been used to improve the defences of a castle which we shall see presently was not really of any great strength.

There are today two ways of approach to the castle, and to my mind by far the more appealing is by the path which climbs steeply from the valley below. If I were taking someone there on a first visit I would take them in winter or early spring when the castle can be seen to stand out majestically on its rugged hilltop. In summer the foliage of the many fine trees obscures this view. Before climbing up to the castle I would take my visitor a little way along the road in

The Castle from the north-east

the valley below towards the Castle Mill. From this point the size and dignity of the ruins are best appreciated. This done I would climb the stile at the foot of the woods, noting on the way the old wall of the Park which comes down from the Lodge a quarter of a mile above us. From the stile the ascent to the castle begins almost imperceptibly with thick, dark woodland all around. Suddenly the gradient becomes steep and soon the visitor gets his first glimpse of the ruins at close quarters. Towering above stands the north-east corner of a gaunt, battlemented castle—its massive mullioned windows still gazing imperiously into the valley as they have done for many a long year. Below them is the rounded St. Margaret's Tower, black and menacing. This was the former home of two powerful families, the Pomeroys and the Seymours, and we have to remember that throughout its centuries of existence no others have owned it. The perilous precipice upon which the castle stands now comes into view on the right hand side. The legend has it that just over there, in days of old, two Pomeroy brothers spurred their blindfolded horses over this sickening drop, riding to certain death rather than surrender their castle to the foes that besieged them. Just before reaching level ground is the site of the old Wishing Tree to which other legends are attached. Suddenly the steep climb is over and we step from the oppressive woodland into the bright daylight once more, and find ourselves on the pleasant lawn before the gatehouse.

The formal approach to the castle is by way of the picturesque drive which descends from the castle Lodge, set high in the red hills of South Devon. Before going through the gate pause to admire the extensive views of the Dartmoor hills which are best seen from a gateway to the left of the Lodge. Here is an ancient barn with a steep-pitched, red-tiled roof. From it the Park wall may be seen running downhill across country into the distance.

Return now to the drive gate; on the left hand side stands a low wall which is of considerable thickness. This is possibly all that still stands of a former gateway described by the Rev. J. B. Swete on his visit in January 1794. He wrote as follows: "I entered the grounds by the side of a gateway which in better days had been a lodge, and a vast circular centre of the Building, now stopt up had clearly been the entrance to the Castle. This, however, had been erected by one of the Seymour family and most probably at the time that the N and E ends of the castle were built for the stile of architecture is the same and there is a manifest similarity in the mouldings of the windows and the surrounding ornaments." Although he left us two watercolour sketches of the castle, unfortunately he left nothing of the now vanished gateway.

The descent to the castle begins steeply, and the drive winds through woods with stately trees on either side. Soon the gradient eases to a gentle downward slope. The banks on either side are carpeted with bluebells in spring, but the approach road is of beauty at any time of the year. No trace of the building is to be seen during our downward journey of about a quarter of a mile, but eventually, after a slight left hand bend, it comes suddenly into view, and we are soon on the green lawn before the gatehouse. In the early nineteenth century, Mrs. Bray, the authoress, tells us that when she visited the castle in 1838 trees were growing right up to the gatehouse and it was hard to recognise it because of thick ivy. Today all this undergrowth has been cleared away and the buildings stand out clearly. To the right stretches the curtain wall and behind it rise the walls of what has been a large and stately mansion. By this second approach the visitor gets the impression that the castle stands at the bottom of a hill. A surprise is then in store for those who walk through the ruins and gaze suddenly upon the precipice beyond. By the first approach, however, it is a hilltop castle which grips the imagination of the visitor, and it is a far more majestic ruin which he sees.

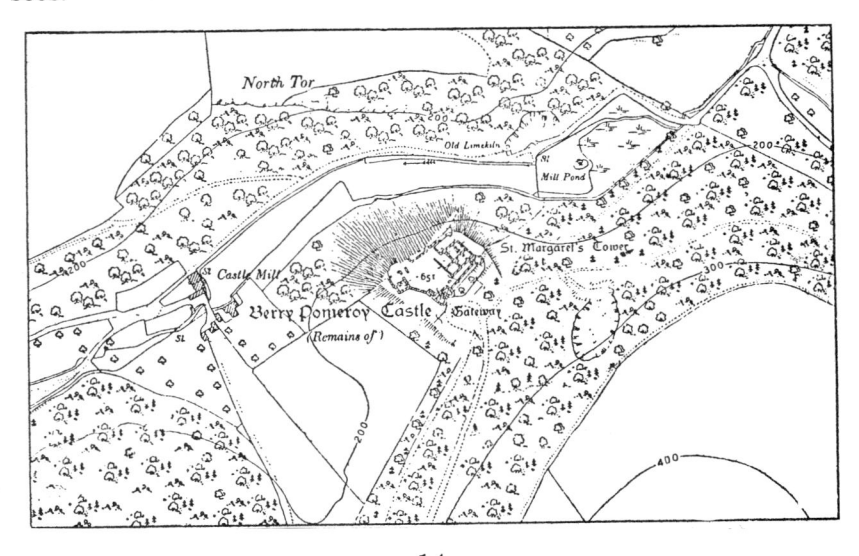

"Why did anyone want a castle just there, and when was it built?" Such are the questions which constantly occur in connection with Berry Pomeroy. The strange thing is that both are difficult questions to answer, for the usual sources tell us nothing of the building of this castle, and it is as late as 1467 before one can point to a written reference to it. Everything about the buildings themselves and the site, too, is open to question. It is generally assumed by writers of all periods that Ralf de la Pomerai erected a castle here after the manor of Beri (amongst many others) had been given to him by William the Conqueror. He is said to have fought at Hastings and much land in the south-west was his reward. In spite of this the noticeboard displayed by the Ministry of the Environment at the castle entrance boldly asserts that we do not have to believe in a Norman castle. Certainly there is no remnant of any such building remaining above ground; and whether excavations yet to come will reveal foundations of a Norman castle of wood or stone no-one can say.

The fact which has not been generally grasped is that the Norman family of de la Pomerai had their home in Normandy at the Chateau Ganne; this lies close to the village of la Pommeraye near Falaise, and it was to be two centuries at least before they sought to make another home on their manor of Beri. Gosselin de la Pomerai gives striking proof of this when he gave land in 1125 to the Norman Abbey of St. Mary du Val, stating that it is situated in front of our home (nostram domum). The chapter on the family stresses the fact that the de la Pomerais were at first absentee landlords. Not until the 13th century do they show any signs of interest in Devon. Then from 1207 onwards, when a deer park was enclosed at Beri, they slowly begin to appear as signatories to local documents and to occupy positions of trust in the county. Even so it was not until 1281 that the manor is first referred to as Berry Pomeroy. Then again we have proof that during this century they lived much at their manor of Tregony in Cornwall, Henry (7) de la Pomerai being born and baptised there in 1265. And when at last they decided to make Berry Pomeroy their permanent home where did they live? Why, surely, at the manor house beside the church which still bears that title. This was the right place for the lord of the manor to be found in both Saxon and Norman days. I am certain that they were still there in 1292 when an important Survey of the demesne was made (see chapter on the de la Pomerai family). It demonstrates that when at

18th century print of Berry Pomeroy Castle by the brothers Buck

Berry the family lived in a simple hall house, typical of the period. The fact that the Park was described in the Survey as "overdone with wild beasts" seems to demonstrate that even in the 13th century the family were not often there to take a personal interest in the estate. The manorhouse today is divided into three houses which surround a central courtyard. I do not doubt that it stands on old foundations. Among the Somerset Papers is an 18th century coloured drawing of the house which appears very different from what it does today. The un-stuccoed walls show the relieving arches of vanished windows which may have been mediaeval. All these are now hidden. The fine barn, however, appears of considerable age and has many features in common with its counterpart at Torre Abbey. It could very well be the grange mentioned in the Survey.

Returning now to the theory that there may have been a Norman castle on the site of the present one, it has to be admitted that this site, naturally defended on three sides by formidable cliffs, could, if a ditch were made on the fourth side, have been a suitable spot for the invading Normans to erect one of their numerous wooden castles. Suppose, too, that they found a ditch already dug for them in antiquity. Such a theory is not beyond the bounds of possibility, because somewhere in the manor there must have been some such stronghold—the "bury" or "burgh" which gave the place its name over a thousand years ago. If not here, then where? We have to admit that unless some such stronghold has been ploughed up long ago there is no other contender for the site. So a wooden castle here in those early post-Conquest days, which were so perilous for the Normans in a hostile land, is a possibility but no more. What we must never do is to think that such a castle was ever the home of the early de la Pomerais.

Assuming therefore that none of the buildings which we see today were built before the 14th century, we come back to the unanswered query—when was the castle built? The usual sources are silent on the subject. There is no royal permission for a fortification here, nor permission to crenellate it. So to our first query we have to add another—why is there no mention? The writer is not the first to be puzzled by the lack of written evidence concerning this castle. After giving much thought to the evidence which the buildings themselves have to offer he had a whole string of further questions to ask. The first point to be settled is why the gatehouse and curtain wall are on a smaller scale than the house. The huge mansion indeed seems at first sight to be pushing the curtain wall into the moat. Why were the fortifications allowed to be dominated by a house— that is if they are to be taken seriously? I shall hope to be able to prove that this house was built entirely by the Pomeroys, and not by the Seymours in Jacobean times as has hitherto been supposed.

If one looks at the gatehouse from the hill immediately opposite, and not from the lawn, its small scale and lack of height and strength are apparent. All admit that the castle had superb natural defences on three sides; but the weak fourth side, so vulnerable at the foot of a downward slope, surely required a really massive gatehouse. Note, too, that there are no battlements to either the towers or the curtain wall, and I am told by masons now at work under the Ministry, that there is no evidence that there ever were any. Prince on the other hand says that there were. Whilst the print engraved by the brothers Buck indeed shows crenellations to the towers of both gatehouse and St. Margaret's tower, were they not doing their best to present the castle with the expected warlike attributes? May they not be simply wishful thinking? Bearing all this in mind one is forced to the perhaps reluctant conclusion that this was never a castle at all in the accepted sense. Instead of a castle it seems that the Pomeroys almost built a folly. But we cannot believe that they were so foolish as this, and the succeeding paragraphs will, I hope, present a reasoned reply to the many questions which now arise.

The house which still stands today is large, and it is unlikely that it was built all at once. When the de la Pomerais at last decided to make Berry their home they would be well aware that the small

INTERIM PLAN of BERRY POMEROY CASTLE

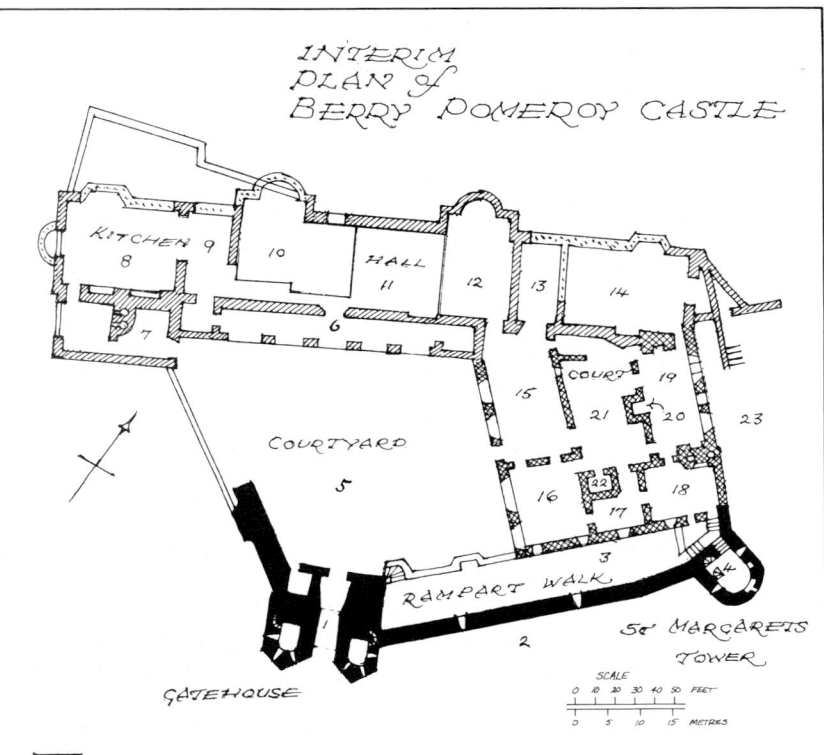

14TH CENTURY FORTIFICATIONS
14TH AND 15TH CENTURY MANOR-HOUSE
LATE 16TH AND EARLY 17TH CENTURY ADDITIONS
VANISHED WALLS
MODERN WALLS

Fortifications of 14th Century
1. Gatehouse with Guardroom over
2. Curtain Wall
3. Rampart Walk
4. St Margaret's Tower

Additions of late 16th and early 17th centuries
5. Courtyard
6. Colonnade
7. Bakery
8. Kitchen
9. Service Room
10. Dining Room
11. Great Hall
12. State Apartments
13. State Apartments
14. State Apartments

Manorhouse of 14th and 15th centuries
15. 14th century Great Hall
16. Service Room
17. Service Room
18. Kitchen
19. Servants' Hall (?)
20. Garde-robes (?)
21. Inner Courtyard
22. Stair-well
23. North Terrace

house by the church was inadequate for their needs. A new manor house should replace the old, they felt. For reasons perhaps more obvious then than now they decided upon the site of the present castle. There was only one big hindrance to an ambitious scheme of building and this was the fact that the family were in debt to the Crown, and had been so ever since Henry (2) de la Pomerai rebelled against King Richard I. Somehow succeeding generations had never managed to raise the money to free the estates from this encumbrance, and at the opening of the 14th century £300 was still owing—a very considerable sum in those days. In the year 1305 the prospects of Henry (7) de la Pomerai improved, for he then inherited a moiety of the manors of Brixham and Harberton. He already held 33 fees in Devon and the manor of Tregony in Cornwall. Nevertheless, had he wanted to build anything so ambitious as a castle it is most unlikely that the King would have permitted it, when he owed so much money to the Crown. We are therefore brought even further forward in time to the first possible date for building a new manor house, and this was in the time of his son, Henry (8). The year 1338 saw a satisfactory end to a long legal wrangle with the Crown over the Valletort estates. The outcome was that Henry (8) was awarded a pension of £40 per annum from the Crown until such time as the King found him estates to the value of £30 per annum. Moreover, we hear no more of the debt to the Crown which was then cancelled.

Henry (8) thus found himself a rich man with estates at last unencumbered. He should have been well able to build the grand new manor house, so much of which still stands today. It is therefore surely safe to assume that by 1340 the house was rising, and it would be completed before the calamity of the Black Death hit Devon in 1348. I shall show presently why I think the plan was U shaped, with two parallel wings flanking a baronial hall. Its plan was similar to that of nearby Compton Castle before the curtain wall there was built. It was, however, on a far larger scale, and was altogether an ambitious building. This house may possibly have had the defence of a moat, but until this has been excavated its age is impossible to assess.

The new manor house of Berry over the next thirty years was to be considerably affected by the long war with France. Landings on the South Devon coast were considered imminent and were a threat to all towns and villages nearby. At Torre Abbey, for instance, permission was given to crenellate in 1348 when the gatehouse was strengthened. It is reasonable to suppose that the Pomeroys felt by no means secure, and so the building of the gatehouse and curtain wall or walls (for there may have been more than we can see today) could have taken place as early as 1350. It is more likely, however, that their building was begun c.1376, for in that year Sir John Pomerey was one of six gentlemen who were commissioned by the King to defend the coast against French landings. This was no panic measure, for in the next year the French did land and burn Rye and Hastings, and there were also assaults on the Isle of Wight and Yarmouth fisheries. So there I think we have good reason for the erection of the slight fortifications of the new manor house at Berry which were later to earn it the title of "castle".

So Sir John seems to have been the one who built the gatehouse with its portcullis and drawbridge—for we are told that the wall bears signs of the housing of the machinery that worked it. To this he added a curtain wall or walls and the tower known as St. Margaret's. If further proof were needed that the house preceded the fortifications, just look at the confused levels at the point where the tower and rampart walk join the house, for they simply do not fit. Then again a window now blocked in the south east wall of the ground floor of the house is actually below the level of the rampart walk, thus demonstrating how when earth and stone was thrown up against the side of the house the window became useless. Neither curtain wall nor gatehouse could have been built an inch further forward—as would have been most desirable—because of the position of the moat. This had to be just where it is to defend the narrow spur on which the buildings stand. To have brought it further forward would have not been possible because of the lie of the land. And this reason applies equally to whether the moat was first constructed in antiquity or in the times of which we are speaking, and also to whether it was a wet or dry moat.

At present we do not know what other buildings may have stood on the site, for several may have been destroyed in the 16th century when the Seymours began their ambitious developments.

There was yet a further enlargement of the Pomeroys' house, and this was the construction of a new wing of four storeys. It joined the ends of the two projecting wings, enclosing an inner courtyard. The interesting thing about this new wing was that the two new walls were freestanding and not joined on to the older house. This work may have been undertaken just after 1433 and before 1446 when

The Pomeroys' Manor House

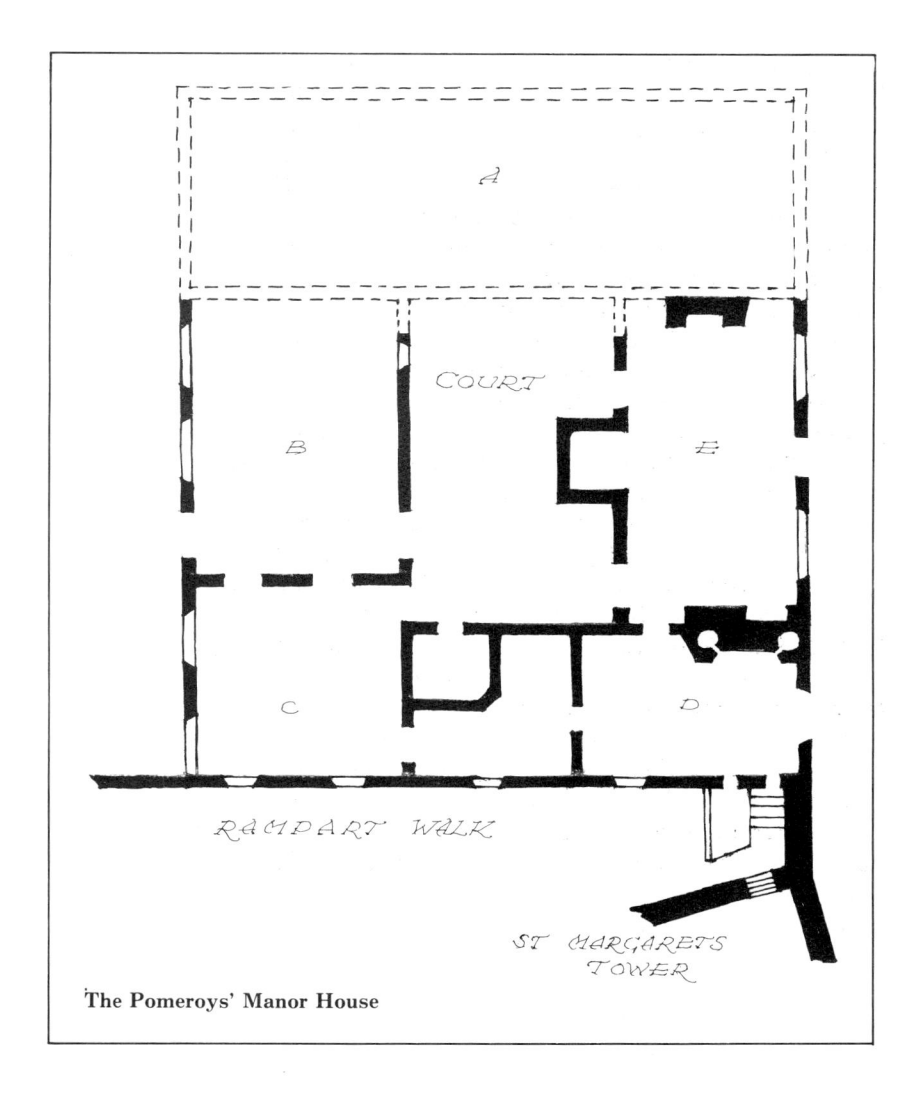

Edward Pomerey of Tregony inherited Berry and a new regime began. Sir John had died childless, and so his cousin Edward was the next heir. He would be a well-to-do man at this time and in a position to enlarge the older house. Sandstone doorways high up in the top storey survive—a complete doorway in the south-east block, but only a half doorway on the opposite side, which opened into the new wing. These two doorways of the 15th century testify to the date of the new extension. So the house had now become roughly square with an inner courtyard. It is unlikely that there were any further additions until the Seymours carried out their great rebuilding programme in late Elizabethan times.

We will next consider the house in detail. "It was all built by the Seymours," we were told, and it was foolish to assert that any parts of it were older. How different is the tale today; for with the ivy stripped away many architectural features have come to light which show that the house is entirely of the Pomeroy period. The Seymours merely adapted the older building to their needs, inserting everywhere the huge granite mullioned windows which admitted plenty of light and which are so characteristic of their work.

Perhaps the south-west facade, which faces onto the courtyard, with its regiment of frowning windows is as good a place as any to begin our survey of the mansion. A close examination will show that it is not quite what it appears to be. The frontage has been refaced with massive blocks of ashlar, several inches thick. At the entrance one can clearly see the Pomeroy walls in situ behind this Jacobean facade. All older features are therefore hidden from view with regard to the exterior. If you crane your neck and consider the upper courses of the wall you will see how the old wall has been heightened above the windows of the top storey. The show battlements, which would continue all round the building, have gone on this side. You will see, too, how between B and C there is an important return wall of considerable strength dividing B from C. Lastly you will observe how the walls between the last two bays on the right of the entrance have been at some time rebuilt with rubble, and badly at that. What happened to the fine ashlar blocks here? Have they been roughly hacked out to make entrances to C, or was it the destructive ivy roots which destroyed this stretch of wall? If so, had repairs not been undertaken, then the safety of the whole of the facade would have been in jeopardy.

If we enter the building beneath the centre bay, then we find ourselves in what looks like a well-proportioned hall, measuring 42ft. by 24ft. 4in. Note that the north-west end wall has entirely gone. An interesting point about the long walls of the hall is that on both sides may be seen the relieving arches of far older windows. We can see here how the square-headed windows of the Seymour rebuilding were jammed into walls never made to receive them. The exterior effect may be satisfactory but the interior workmanship shows much crude adaptation. Particularly amazing in this respect is the final window of the lowest storey at the north-west end. Here, for reasons best known only to the rebuilders, the upper courses of the old wall were never properly removed to make way for the new window; they hang down with jagged edges, suspended in mid air at least a foot below the transom of the new window. Such sorry work would never have been tolerated in one of the important rooms, and one can only suppose that this lower floor was put to menial uses. With leaded glass in the windows the outside effect would have been satisfactory; but what a strange imperfection to find in so important a house! We shall see that it is only one of many.

The hint of a cross passage and two service doors suggest that this was the hall of the Pomeroys' manor house. In the south-east wall are joist holes for a wooden gallery over a screens passage, with a door leading to C at second floor level. Note that no hearth is visible today. It is not likely to have been at the vanished dais end of the hall, so possibly there was a central hearth. This is a thing which future excavation may reveal. Note next how in this spacious hall there were corbels which once supported a fine roof. One corbel remains yet, but gaps in the walls show where others once were. It is doubtful if the roof was as high as the present walls. One rather feels that the top storey should not be there and that it spoils the proportions of the hall. It may very well have been a Seymour addition. Once again we can compare this building with Compton Castle where the height of the Great Hall roof is much lower than its flanking wings. Note, too, how there is a fireplace in the end room of the top storey; it appears to be the only one in the whole block, so to whatever use did the Seymours put this wing? As there are no signs of return walls anywhere, the upper floors may have been long galleries connecting the grand apartments of the palatial new house with the many bedchambers in the old.

We will next consider A, a wing which the Seymours entirely demolished, apart from the wall which later contained the fireplaces in the north-west wall of E. It has already been mentioned how the long walls of E are, surprisingly, free-standing. These massive walls are thus standing between the older blocks A and C. It is quite impossible to imagine that the end wall at the north-west end of E was also free-standing, and so it is reasonable to suppose that it once formed the outside south-east wall of A. The chimney and its atten-

N.W. end of Inner Courtyard

dant fireplaces are thus all that now remains of A. The great point to notice is this—it is in line with the rest of the building, but not with the adjacent walls of the newer Seymour house. Notice, too, that if produced, the vanished wall would meet the end wall of the Great Hall, which is just what it should have done. The foundations of the walls of A may still lie in situ awaiting the trowels of a further excavation.

The corresponding wing to A on the opposite side of the building is C and D—two sections separated by a dividing wall. This corner of the house is full of interesting features and not a few puzzling ones. At first sight it might be thought that C was built first—a four storeyed tower with an exterior staircase at M. However, consideration of the quite unbroken masonry of the south-eastern face of this wing is against this theory. It shows no sign of a join anywhere and so we are forced back upon the fact that C and D are contemporaneous. The curious stairwell we will consider presently. Taking C first, we note that the lower floor connected with B, the Great Hall, by two doors. A feature to notice in the one on the north-east side is a fragment of worked granite still in position. It is all that is left of a typical 14th century arched doorway.* Behind the facade are two relieving arches of older windows similar to those in the Great Hall. The first floor rooms in both C and D seem to have had low ceilings and small windows when compared with the lofty rooms and huge windows of the Seymour period

---

*A blocked 14th century doorway in the same style is still in situ below the present floor level in the north corner of the castle at "Pomeroy's Leap" (see illustration on (p.94).

which grace the two upper floors. The fireplace, too, on the first floor is small and humble and I much wonder whether this first floor did not contain servants' quarters. To support this idea note that the large staircase bypasses this first floor altogether.

Coming now to the second floor, we have what was evidently one of the principal apartments of the Pomeroys' house—a room lit with windows on two sides and containing a fine fireplace arched over with large sandstone blocks. There are yet one or two corbels remaining at this level, showing how beams once supported timber ceilings. On the third floor the fireplace is on the north-west side. So there are two chimneys in C, part of whose stacks still stand. A fine feature is a sandstone doorway of the fifteenth century which is perched high up in the wall of the third storey. It connects C and D.

We consider next D, which is one of the most intriguing parts of the whole building, for it is full of enigmas. The most conspicuous object on ground floor level is a large hearth with ovens on both sides. Clearly it was at some period a kitchen, but the chimney is not shared by any of the other floors. It is built out from the wall, and is not a part of its construction. It has its own chimney stack which is almost touching another stack serving the fireplaces in the southeast wall of E. Adjoining the second stack is yet a third which served the fireplaces in the upper floors of D. So we have three chimney stacks alongside each other. No one would have designed such a melée of chimneys in a house where only the best craftsmanship was to be expected! Clearly the chimneys represent three different periods of building. The last mentioned must be the oldest, for it belongs to the flues from the huge fireplaces on the 2nd and 3rd floors which the 14th century builders constructed. The centre chimney, serving the newer block E, will date from the next century. But we cannot be sure of the intruding kitchen chimney. Two possibilities spring to mind; firstly, the servants' hall may have been on the ground floor of E, which has fireplaces at each end. There are no signs that this large room was ever divided into two smaller ones. The number of servants employed in this spacious house must have been considerable, and for them to have had an independent kitchen inserted when E was built is quite feasible. On the other hand, when the castle was abandoned at the close of the 17th century, we know from Sir Walter Farquhar's story (see p.116) that the steward of the estate was still living in a few habitable rooms. This type of kitchen hearth with its ovens was common in

Devon well into the 19th century. Plaster still adheres to the walls of the first floor rooms in many places, and one has the feeling that this was the last part of the castle to be lived in. So was the chimney, with its large fireplace, built for the steward's kitchen?

To the left of this chimney and high up in the third storey is a blocked window which once looked out to the north-west. When the later wing E was constructed it would, of course, become useless and be built up. Amongst the Seymour Papers in the Record Office at Trowbridge, there is a book of lithographs, one of which depicts this wing D. At first floor level, beside the chimney, is a spiral stair which can be seen again emerging on the next floor. There is not a trace of this today, neither is any disturbance in the masonry of the wall to be seen. It is, I think, artist's licence. The title of the print is "State Rooms".

Notice next the huge mullioned windows of the Seymour rebuilding which gave glorious views from the top floors. Notice, too, how the windows on the first floor are only of two lights and of little importance, thus giving strength to the theory that this was the servants' floor. In the south-east wall at ground floor level is the blocked window already mentioned. Since it is now below the level of the rampart walls, it surely gives more than a hint that the latter was constructed after the house. It may have been lit by a shaft, but this would have admitted but little light, especially when one considers that there are indications that the rampart walk was once roofed in.

Another curious feature of the wall is a nicely arched, narrow doorway of the late 14th century. It has a shaft of what is probably Beer stone on one side, but on the other the arch is merely supported by rubble. Can such a doorway be said to be in situ? Or has it been brought here from another part of the building? It opens from the rampart walk into the first floor rooms, and suggests that the guard may have had quarters there. In the north-east corner a flight of stairs leads to the St. Margaret's Tower and also to the rampart walk. I have already drawn attention to the strange jumble of stairs and levels in this corner, which can only be explained by different periods of construction.

Before leaving D, stand by the fireplace, and then turn to consider those projecting walls in the right hand corner which once housed a wide staircase. This was no awkward spiral stair, but a much later spacious staircase of generous proportions, the impressions of whose stairs are to be seen yet upon the walls. Attention has already been drawn to the fact that no doorway from it opens onto the humble, low ceilinged first floor—good evidence, surely, for this being the servants' floor.

The building of the free-standing walls of E mark another and later period in the story of the Pomeroys' manor house. It was possibly carried out by Edward Pomeray, an affluent man, who died in 1446. This wing of four storeys has several interesting features to notice. First is the little room hollowed out in the thickness of the walls between E and D, and just to the left of the fireplace. It has a small square window of sandstone. Several suggestions have been made as to the use to which this room was put. (1) that this was where the Pomeroys hid their treasure; (2) that it was a garde-robe; (3) that it was a place for smoking bacon etc.; (4) that a turn-spit used it when at work, watching the roast in the hearth below him. The large projecting bay on the south-west side with its series of two-light sandstone windows also poses difficulties. It looks as though it should have contained a staircase, yet there is no trace that there ever was one. There ought, surely, to have been a door on the ground floor, but again there never was. Inside there are traces of a blocked window instead. Did the bay perhaps contain a series of garde-robes? Quite a likelihood, one would think, as there is a complete absence of them elsewhere. On this south-west exterior wall there is much sandstone in evidence in the two light windows, and traces of a doorway at the north-west end. From the courtyard may be seen part of a fine chimney buttress belonging to the oldest chimney in D. Most of it was unfortunately obscured when the south-west wall of E was built up against it. Lastly, turn to admire the exterior wall of the Great Hall. The stones comprising the relieving arches of one of its old windows may be clearly seen from here.

So the house which we have been considering, although it may be of different periods, was all constructed by the Pomeroys. It will date from the 14th to 15th centuries, and was at that time one of the largest manor houses in Devon. We should always remember that there may have been even more of it beneath the walls of the later Seymour mansion. For instance an old print of the kitchen and bakehouse block on the opposite side of the courtyard calls it "Elizabeth Tower". So was it possibly so-called because of its proximity to rooms in which Lady Elizabeth Pomeray lived in her widowhood? The heir to her husband Sir Richard's estates was Edward (2) who was under age at the time of his father's death. His guardian, John Sapcotes, received in 1497 a Grant of the "keeping of the lands of Sir Richard" (Pat. Rolls 1494-1509, 108). In it the share of the Lady Elizabeth in the castle and capital messuage are precisely set forth—"her third of the honor and castle of Beri" was to be "a great chamber beyond the castle gate with a cellar on the left of the gate, with two chambers beyond and belonging to the said great chamber, a kitchen, a larder house and a chamber beyond the kitchen." Now if anyone tries to discover these rooms in the ruins of today they are faced with insuperable difficulties, for there is no great chamber beyond the castle gate, and surely one old lady was not allotted the main kitchen? It all rather suggests vanished buildings which once stood on the left hand side of the courtyard.

The Grant continues by saying that the good lady also had her third share of the capital messuage of Bury Pomeray, and gives a further list of rooms which included a "pantry, buttery and all chambers beyond and under the said pantry and buttery up to the Stuerdischambre with a moiety of a Bakehouse, Bruhouse, kechyn and Lardehouse". Some writers have looked for all this at the castle and immediately got into deep waters. Why should Lady Elizabeth have wanted a half share in another kitchen and offices when she already had all she wanted at the castle? The capital messuage referred to is, of course, not the castle but the old manor house by the church. It was of this that she was to have one third. Her rooms extended to the "Stuerdischambre". He, no doubt, had rooms in the house as well, and they shared the kitchen. The other third may very well have been taken up by the courthouse of the manor and its offices. But the hint which the Grant gives of a vanished block of buildings at the castle is not to be easily dismissed.

THE GATEHOUSE

It has already been mentioned that the gatehouse could have been built c.1376 by John Pomerey. He certainly had the means to do it, and the added spur of being one of those in charge of the local defences against the French. The labour, too, would be to hand, for the Black Death, which was at its height in the middle of the century, was abating by then. The invading forces, one would expect, could not have been of really great strength, and the gatehouse with its portcullis, machicolation and drawbridge would have had decided nuisance value. For all its meagre size its proportions are pleas-

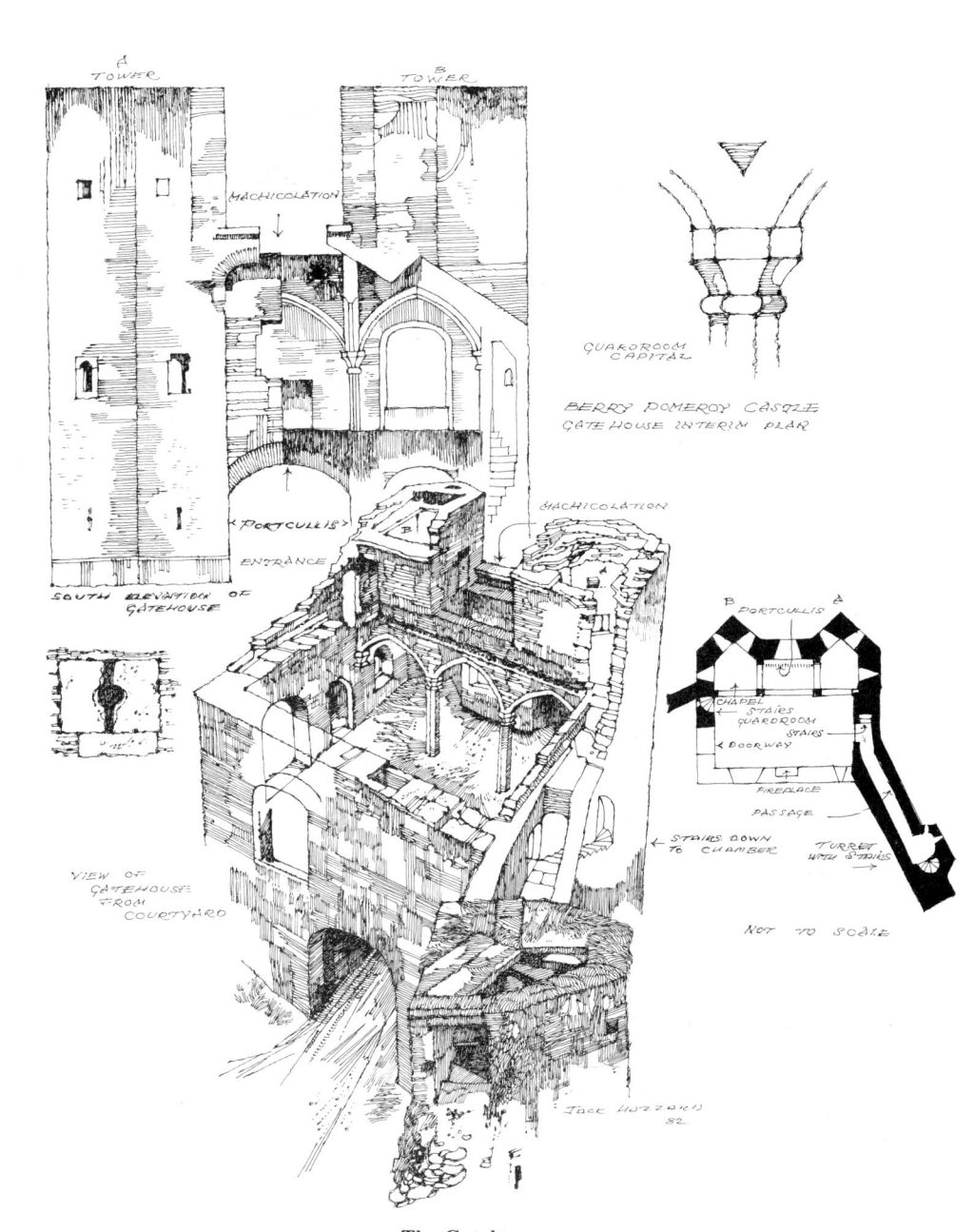

The Gatehouse

ing; the flanking hexagonal towers are of decided dignity, looking much more forbidding than they really are. Since the frontage of each has two faces, bowmen could control a greater range. The dimensions of the gatehouse are as follows:- Height of towers 42ft., height of intervening wall 32ft.; height of entrance archway 11ft.7in.; courtyard archway 9ft.10in.; width of entrance 8ft.5in. Note how low the archway is. Could a horseman in armour with helmet, crest and lance have ridden through? It must be remembered, of course, that our ancestors were men of lesser stature than ourselves. The surface of the entrance is rugged, for it is right down on the naked rock, and has quite a steep gradient as it ascends into the courtyard. At some time it was extended inwards by 12ft. A rough and perhaps intentionally awkward entrance. In the grand days of the Seymours did they deign to use it? Or did they bypass it by a grand new approach on the south-west side?

The towers are of three storeys with the remains of parapets on top. The Bucks' print does not show the central machicolation, thus demonstrating how little some of the details in the early prints of the castle are to be relied upon. Below the central window is a small square stone said by Prince and others to have had the arms of Pomeroy carved upon it. Unfortunately this has weathered away and now only the stone remains.

A careful examination shows how the entrance has been extended towards the courtyard. This suggests that the wall above it was rebuilt and placed a few feet further in that direction too. We do not know when this alteration was carried out. At the end of the passage, on the right hand side, is a blocked entry, possibly a door or perhaps merely an aperture in which stood a sentry in bygone days.*

Ascending now by a stone spiral stair we reach the rampart walk where, on our right, a plainly arched doorway leads into the former guardroom. Another staircase to the left leads upward to the first floor, but the doorway to this level is now blocked. The so-called guardroom has one important feature which immediately catches the eye, for an arcade of three bays runs right across the room. The arches spring from octagonal columns with plain capitals. The ar-

---

*Opened in 1982. Earth and loose stones were all that was to be seen. Before the extension of the gatehouse the spiral stair to the rampart walk was possibly situated here.

cade is joined to the front wall of the gatehouse by two further arches which spring from the same two columns. All is of granite, and the effect is quite ecclesiastical. In the north-west corner is a spacious fireplace and chimney. Spiral stairways on both sides of the room lead down to "dungeons" at the foot of the towers. Beyond the fireplace a passage leads to the west. This is the only roofed passage still remaining: it leads to a very broken stairway which gives access to the top of a small, ruinous tower. It is possible that the original curtain wall had an extension from here towards the kitchens. In the centre of the passage is an opening which some say was a garde-robe. In the centre of the guardroom and immediately beneath the central window is the aperture down which the portcullis was once dropped. The roof of the guardroom and towers has quite gone, but one can understand how the arcade was needed to support both it and the low walls of the backs of the towers.

Now, amid the warlike atmosphere of the guardroom something has recently been discovered which causes us to rethink our ideas as to the latter use of this first floor room. On the north-east wallface of the south-eastern tower a large ochre fresco has been uncovered, after being obscured for centuries by moss and fungus. This almost miraculous survival, part of which was first noticed by a visitor and fortunately reported, is now being lovingly restored by the expert skill of Polish-born Mrs. Krystina Barakal, a well-known authority on such things. The fresco depicts an Adoration of the Magi, and is about six feet from the ground. The painting is considered to be of very superior workmanship; it is thought to date from the late fifteenth century, and, considering all things, is in a fair state of preservation. The figures of the three wise men are on the left of the scene, and are large in proportion to those of the Virgin and Child. She is seated. Unfortunately the head of Jesus is obliterated. So is the whole figure of St. Joseph. On the extreme right, and in a small panel, are shown the head and shoulders of a man and woman, no doubt the owners of the castle at that time. Above them is a highly stylized castle with heavily battlemented towers. It would be intended that it should typify, not of course portray, Berry Pomeroy Castle. The very large container of Caspar's gift of gold is curious. Though partly obscured, it resembles a large chalice with a tall lid. Melchior's frankincense is in a silver thurible, but Balthazzar's gift of myrrh cannot now be seen.

It is very easy to jump to conclusions and say that the guardroom must by the fifteenth century have become the castle chapel. Imagination then comes to one's aid, and we see an altar standing centrally below the window, whilst a wood floor has obscured the portcullis aperture. Both towers could have been adorned with frescoes and become little oratories. The orientation of south-east would be within the bounds of possibility. But we must remember that one fresco does not make a chapel. At that period it was a common thing to adorn the walls of a house in such a way, and religious subjects were common. Apart from this one thing there is no other object to give support to the chapel theory. No piscina survives, for instance, and it must be remembered, too, that the church-like arcade might have been built in any 14th century secular edifice. Then again the staircase, doors, and the passage entrance, together with the fireplace, all militate against the theory of a chapel here. Certainly there is no mention in the Bishop's Registers of any chapel at the castle ever being licensed. So at present we should not try to read too much into the discovery of the splendid fresco.

THE RAMPART WALK AND ST. MARGARET'S TOWER

The length of the Rampart Walk from the Guardroom door to the steps which lead down to St. Margaret's Tower is 104ft. Its width 15ft.6in. and the walk is at a height of 6ft.3in. above the courtyard. The only signs of fortification are two embrasures in the curtain wall 5ft.6in. and 4ft.9in. in width. They have widely-splayed jambs and their slit openings could have been used for crossbows or perhaps for the later musket type of weapon. The curtain wall rises to a height of 7ft.6in. above the rampart walk and 16ft.8in. above ground level; about half way along there is the suggestion of the spring of an arch which once spanned the walk. So we have more than a hint that the walk was formerly roofed. A further clue is provided by the large window beside the courtyard stairs. If the walk was unroofed then this window was useless. The walk ends close to St. Margaret's Tower with a wall on either side of a flight of six steps; they lead to a kind of landing just below the first floor level of the tower. On the left of the landing stands the narrow doorway described in the survey of the house, which enters it on the first floor of D. Ahead, a wide spiral stair leads down to the left, descending to the ground floor of D. To the right of the landing one step led onto the threshold of the second floor of St. Margaret's Tower. No fur-

Rampart Walk — **looking towards guardroom**

ther comment is needed here with regard to the awkward way in which this corner was contrived.

St. Margaret's Tower is the only remaining round tower, but there may at one time have been more if the curtain wall continued on the north-western side of the castle. The print by the brothers Buck shows this tower as much higher than it is now, and with crenellation. This may have been wishful thinking on their part, but there

Rampart Walk — looking towards St Margaret's Tower

certainly does appear to be remains of a narrow stair on the right, but who can say whether it led to another storey or merely to the roof of the tower at its present height? The second floor room was fitted with a fireplace and a pleasing window of the 14th century, containing three lights. The first floor room also has a small fireplace and square windows. From here steps lead down to a comfortless cell, and it was there, so the legend has it, that the luckless Lady Margaret Pomeroy was imprisoned by her jealous sister, Eleanor.

The Rev. John Prince remarks that several gentlemen held their land from St. Margaret's Tower. By this I can only assume that he meant that the actual charters granting leases etc. were issued here. This suggests that the Pomeroys used the second floor room as a business room or office. I had hoped to find among the Pomeroy papers charters ending with the words "Given at St. Margaret's Tower", but none such have so far appeared, though I inspected a great many. The common ending was "Given at Byry", followed by the date. Our friend Prince was the first to use the prefix "Saint" in connection with this tower. Whether deserved by Lady Margaret or not, the title has stuck through the centuries and we cannot attempt to change it now.

On the right of the staircase from the courtyard, as we face the guardroom door, are the scanty remains of a further spiral stair. Whilst this may only have given access to the roof of the rampart walk, it does give a hint of a second storey. We have already noticed close by what appears to have been a large bay window at the guardroom end of the walk. Notice how this bay continues right down to ground level. Could it have been the shaft of a garde-robe, with the window above it?

Before leaving the rampart walk look up and admire the strength of the great south-east wall of the house. The masonry has stood the test of time well and appears much stronger than the curtain wall. Notice how massive is the hoodmoulding of the windows which the Seymours inserted. Notice also in contrast the poorness of those plain windows of two lights which serve the first floor. The windows seem to be in design akin to those facing onto the inner courtyard. The only break anywhere in this solid wall face is a filling-in, high up near the south-west end. In shape it resembles a door, but the improbability of any such thing just here suggests that it was a repair carried out at some time to the ageing wall.

St Margaret's Tower

The Seymour Mansion

THE COLONNADE

Until the recent excavations took place the courtyard was covered by a disorderly tangle of fallen stones, undergrowth and uneven turf. Nowhere could the original level be seen, except towards the gatehouse where the naked rock showed itself. Towards the kitchens a great mound of debris had to be climbed over, whilst a lesser mound was up against the north-west end of the facade. It was the object of the excavations of 1979-80 to expose the floor of the courtyard and clear the debris. No one could have expected such rewarding results, yet had the old writer John Prince been taken at his word the emergence of the graceful Jacobean colonnade from beneath the debris would have been a foregone conclusion. It has re-appeared just as he described it, and consisted of five bays with rounded arches resting on pilasters and pediments, all in Beer stone. The stones of only one complete arch, however, were disovered, the rest having been removed from the site at some time over the centuries. Drawings prepared from the fragments so far rescued show a handsome structure in the Jacobean style. Fragments of tinted glass have come to light showing that leaded diamond panes were used in the windows. Whilst the whole of the colonnade could have been glazed in the style of a cloister, yet it is considered far more likely that glazing was only used for the windows opening into the

Great Hall of the Seymours' new house. At each end are rectangular spaces, separated from the colonnade by a wall. These may have contained staircases, but at present their exact use has not been established.

Prince mentioned seats of stone, backed with escallop shells, where the company might rest when "aweary". Two of these are still in situ and were found at the north-west end. Those at the opposite end have unfortunately gone. The shells mentioned have also gone. Their design, however, can easily be reconstructed, for they are typical of their period. Such stone seats are to be seen, for instance at Cothelstone Manor in Somerset, where they will be found in the walls of the Lodge. There they are single seats, however, but the Berry Pomeroy ones are double. There are masons' marks scratched upon them and also crude emblems probably done by children.

On the south-west side of the courtyard a large outcrop of raised rock shows itself within a few feet of the colonnade. One cannot but

The author and his wife sitting on seats in the
Jacobean colonnade uncovered in 1981

wonder why so primitive a feature was allowed to remain amidst the surrounding grandeur, but it must be remembered that the house itself was never quite completed, and so the clearance of the rock was one of the things left to the last, and then never done at all.

It will be interesting to see whether the rest of the courtyard was paved or whether, like the passage beneath the gatehouse, its floor was the naked rock. It is worth recording that once during an extreme summer drought a circular depression showed itself before the entrance to the gatehouse, and a little to the left. It is thought that it might be a covered-in well.

THE KITCHEN AND BAKEHOUSE

The kitchen has two large fireplaces measuring 11ft.6in. and 9ft., one with an oven. So crude and primitive do the undressed arches of these fireplaces appear that it is tempting to assign them to the Pomeroy period. A glance at the plan, however, shows that the massive chimney breast is a part of the south-east wall of the Seymour extension which stretches from one end of the castle site to the other; it is of considerable thickness. The Pomeroy kitchen must also have stood on the left hand side of the Courtyard, for it is mentioned in the Grant of 1497 as a part of the dower of Lady Elizabeth Pomeray.

Both kitchen and bakehouse were lit by large windows, and the outside approach was by a doorway on the south-western side of the building. It was reached by semi-circular steps which are still in situ. A partial excavation has seen all debris and fallen stone cleared from the kitchen, but the actual floor level has yet to be reached. Fragments of 17th century Totnes ware were found. The spaciousness of the kitchen can now be appreciated.

On the right hand side of the larger hearth, and at first floor level, is an intriguing cavity in the thickness of the wall. It is not a hearth, and in place of a ceiling are several pieces of timber; they appear to be original and are in excellent condition. The reputed story that the castle was destroyed by fire is contradicted here, for the wood shows no sign of ever being subject to fire. The use of this snug spot, which would always be warm from the fires below, is debateable. We may be sure it was put to good use.

This is perhaps the time to mention that the actual name of one of the cooks who presided over the Pomeroy's kitchen is known. His name was Negelle, which suggests that even then French chefs were in demand. A charter in the Wiltshire County Record Office at Trowbridge (201.Box 2) tells of a lease from Sir Henry de la Pomeraye to Negelle, "my cook, of a tenement and land in the manor of Stockelegh". Our cook, who must have been a man of means, paid a rent of 12d. a quarter to his master for this. Most unfortunately the charter is undated, but its style suggests the 14th century.

THE STATE ROOMS

The whole of the north-western stretch of the clifftop on which the castle stands was occupied by the Jacobean addition which the Seymours added to the Pomeroys' manor house. In the process older buildings may have been demolished. It was laid out at a different angle to the old house so that every inch of space on the restricted site could be made use of. The length was about 220ft., but the width could only be 35ft. This new wing, facing north-west, must have looked most impressive from the valley below which it would dominate. The main doorway was in the centre of a Jacobean colonnade which had five arches resting on six pillars. The door led into a new Great Hall with a dining room beyond. To the north-east were two more state rooms. But the magnificent Great Parlour was on the first floor and the remains of its huge fireplace are yet to be seen. The imposing doorway to this spacious room is still in position. Bedchambers may have taken up the rest of the room on the first floor, but we must remember that the Great Hall may have had a lofty roof taking in the first storey. Staircases and galleries possibly ascended from both sides of the hall. The lack of more fireplaces over the only one left suggests that this new wing was no more than two storeys in height. With its loftier rooms, however, it was the same height as the old house with which it was connected. The remaining walls are of great strength and the stacks of masonry still standing would support large mullioned windows on either side. It is, of course, fruitless to attempt to describe the vanished building. We must try to see it through the eyes of the one eyewitness who knew the castle and loved it; this was the former Vicar of Berry Pomeroy, the Reverend John Prince. He wrote thus in 1701 in his "Worthies of Devon": "It was a castle, standing a mile distant towards the east from the parish church of Biry aforesaid.

What it was in its antique form, can hardly be calculated from what at present remains standing, which is only the front, facing south in a direct line, of about 60 cloth-yards in length. The gate standeth towards the west end of the front, over which, carved in moor-stone, yet remaineth Pomeroy's arms. (viz. Or, a lion rampant Gules within a bordure engrailed Sable). It had heretofore a double portcullis, whose entrance is about 12 foot in height and 30 foot in length; which gate is turretted and embattled, as are the walls yet standing, home to the east thereof where answereth, yet in being, a tower called St. Margaret's, from which several gentlemen in this county anciently held their lands. Within this is a large Quadrangle, at the North and East whereof, the honourable family of Seymour (whose Possession it is) built a magnificent Structure at the Charges, as Fame relates it, upward of Twenty Thousand Pounds, but never brought it to perfection: for the West side of the Quadrangle was never begun; what was finished may thus be described: Before the door of the great Hall was a noble Walk, whose length was the breadth of the Court, arch'd over with curiously carved Free stone, supported in the forepart, by several stately pillars of the same Stone of great dimensions, after the Corinthian Order, standing on Pedestals, having Cornices or Friezes finely wrought; behind which were placed in the Wall several Seats of Frieze-stone also, cut into the form of an Escallop-shell, in which the Company, when aweary, might repose themselves.

"The Apartments within were very splendid; especially the Dining Room which was adorn'd besides Paint, with Statues and Figures cut in Alabaster, with admirable Art and Labour; but the Chimney-piece of polished Marble, curiously engraven, was of great Cost and Value. Many other of the Rooms were well adorned with Moldings and Fretwork; some of whose Marble Clavils were so delicately fine, that they would reflect an Object true and lively from a great distance. In short, the number of the Apartments of the whole may be collected hence, if Report be true that it was a good Days Work for a Servant but to open and shut the Casements belonging to them. Notwithstanding which 'tis now demolished, and all this Glory lieth in the Dust, buried in its own Ruines there being nothing standing but a few broken Walls, which seem to mourn their own approaching Funerals."

It is to be understood that as further excavations are pending the Ministry of the Environment has not as yet produced a final plan of the buildings. The plan appended can therefore only be a revision of the old plan in the light of recent excavations. It must be regarded as an interim plan and no more. It shows how the new building was symmetrical in style—its salient points being two large bow windows and two smaller bay windows which broke up the north-west facade. As in other buildings of the period these great bow windows probably extended to the upper storey.

In addition to the new block, the Seymours completely transformed the existing house, inserting large mullioned windows of granite with heavy transoms and hood-moulding. The whole was probably surmounted by show battlements which remain only at the south-east corner. Altogether the Berry Pomeroy Castle which Devonians of the 17th century saw was a large and stately house with few rivals in the county at that time.

The stone used throughout the buildings is from the South Hams with the notable exception of the Dartmoor granite used so extensively in the windows and a few doorways. I am grateful for the opinion of Mr. R. Treseder, a lifelong geologist, who has listed the use of the various stone and the quarries from which it comes. Gatehouse: the darkest slate from Charlton Quarry, the lighter from Englebourne Quarry near Harbertonford. Sandstone, which contains quartzite, from Lower Blagdon. Granite window frames with the exception of the small southwest window which is Beerstone, badly weathered away. Curtainwall: a limestone foundation, but the main wall has very irregular courses and is a possible rebuilding. St. Margaret's Tower: nicely built Pomeroy work of Englebourne slate. Seymour block of slate and limestone. Courtyard: the recently unearthed pedestals of the colonnade are of Beer stone resting on granite foundations.

To sum up, the evidence points to the older house being built between 1300 and 1340. The gatehouse, curtain wall and St. Margaret's Tower came later, say 1350-1376. Next in order was the 15th century addition at E, the work probably being carried out by 1446. Lastly came the building by the Seymours of the great new wing and complete remodelling of older house. The colonnade also dates from the same era.

CHAPTER 2
Berry under the Pomeroys
(c.1066-1548)

The family was from Normandy and took its name from the village of La Pommeraye near Falaise. A castle there, which became the family home, was known as Le Chateau Ganne. No less than 19 generations were to own the manor of Berry which later became known as Berry Pomeroy. The purpose of this chapter is to provide a brief sketch of each owner. The spelling of the name of Pomeroy has varied over the centuries. The Latin form in the Exchequer Domesday survey was de Pomeria, whilst in the Exeter Domesday it was de la Pomerai, and later Poumerai; but in the 15th century this was dropped for a more English version which was Pomeray. Later it changed to Pomerey and finally to Pomeroy or Pumerey.

Before the Conquest the manor of Beri was owned by the Saxon Alric or Alricius, who also held Cockington. Like so many Saxon owners of property he was ejected by the Normans and is not heard of again. The manor at that time was a prosperous one, consisting of two hides; it was worth £16.

I.Ralf de la Pomerai
(d.c.1102)

From the time of the Domesday Survey until 1548 the names of every one of the lords of Berry Pomeroy are known — and in most cases much more than just the names. It is obvious that least will be known of the earliest generations. It is popularly supposed that Ralf de la Pomerai came over with William the Conqueror and fought at the Battle of Hastings. He was richly rewarded with land in Devon, of which the manor of Beri was a part. Powley, the most able of those who have written on the subject, gives as evidence the quotation from Du Chesne's "Historiae Normannorum (Tabula — Battail Abbay) 1619 App. 1023". If Du Chesne's work is reliable then we have no reason to suppose that Ralf did not accompany the Conqueror, but there is one writer who does not think he did and that is J. Scanes (see T.D.A. 1923). He thinks that there is insufficient evidence to support Ralf's claim, and considers that he came over later, doing service to the Conqueror at the Siege of

Exeter in 1068. Here he acquired six houses on which he refused to pay the customary dues. Scanes points out that he may have been no more than an ordinary man-at-arms who grabbed what he could get. The Domesday record under Codrintona describes him as a soldier ("Hanc tenet Radulfus quidem miles") and under Aedstone as "Radulfus quondam miles". Prince, writing in 1741, rather backs up this idea by saying that the family of Pomeroy was not very noble in origin, but became so by alliances, once with royal blood and several times with daughters of peers. If Ralf's blood was not as blue as it might have been we can be certain that by the time of the Domesday Survey he really did own 57 manors in Devon and 2 in Somerset. Of these Beri was the richest, Ashcombe and Bradworthy coming next. Its calculated acreage was 2650. The Exeter Domesday account of the manor of Beri is as follows:— "Radulf has a manor called Beri, which Alric held on the day etc., and it was assessed for geld on 2 hides. These can be ploughed by 25 ploughs. Of these Radulf has in demesne 1 hide and 4 ploughs and the villeins have 1 hide and 17 ploughs. There Radulf has 45 villeins and 17 bordars and 16 serfs and 8 head of cattle and 17 swine and 560 sheep and 100 acres of wood and 10 of meadow and 41 of pasture. This is worth £12 and when Radulf received it it was worth £16". The picture is of a well developed and populous manor where sheep farming was active.

If Ralf did not fight at Hastings he must have rendered the King signal service in other ways — perhaps, as we have said, at the Siege of Exeter — for he would appear to have been the 5th largest baronial tenant in Devon, holding no less than 57 manors. We do not know whom he married, but he had two sons, William and Gosselin. He also had a brother, William Capra, who held 42 manors in Devon; so he, too, was a considerable land-owner. Note that he does not style himself de la Pomerai, thus showing that the name was not as yet regarded as a surname. There was also a sister, Beatrix, whom the brothers had as a sub-tenant. There is nothing else that we know of Ralf, except the fact that he must have been dead by the year 1102 when William, his son, alienated Beri.

There is no evidence to support the idea that Ralf built a castle on the site of the present one, yet one after another of the old writers say that he did. The concensus of expert opinion now is that the castle was begun in the 14th century; no existing walls are considered earlier than that date. Than again there is no suggestion that Ralf ever resided at Beri — no records of his doing anything at all in this corner of Devon after the Siege of Exeter. The most one can say is that he could have built a wooden castle, such as many of the Norman barons did, and used the present site; but we do not have to believe even this.

So the first Norman owner of Beri is a shadowy figure of whose actions we cannot be sure. The idea that he was an adventurous man-at-arms who cashed in on the opportunities afforded by the Conquest is attractive. No one can say that he did not make the most of those opportunities. There is one thing of which we may be sure — by the time of the Domesday Survey Ralf would be regarded as a baron, for in the reign of King William I it was a term which began to be applied to any tenant-in-chief by reason of his tenure.

2. William de la Pomerai
(d.*c.*1104)

William succeeded to his father's estates, and only two things are known about him; firstly that he alienated Beri to the Abbey of St. Peter at Gloucester, and secondly that he had a son named Ethelward. The name, being Saxon, is of interest and suggests that William may have married a Saxon. Ethelward is credited by Leland to have refounded Buckfast Abbey. This is an error, however, which has been perpetuated by other historians. The late Dom John Stephan in his "History of Buckfast Abbey" pours scorn on the assertion, concluding "The Pomeroys never had any part to play in the foundation, or even the development of Buckfast, and it is only through the unfortunate lapse of John Leland that their name has ever come into the picture". Ethelward did not succeed to his father's estates and is not heard of again. Both he and his father are therefore rather enigmatic figures and we know very little about them.

Scanes does not consider that William parted with the whole of his manor to the monks of Gloucester; he gives no proof for this assertion, however.

3. Gosselin de la Pomerai
(still living 1137-41)

He was the brother of William and apparently the second son of Ralf. What had happened to his nephew Ethelward, who one would have expected to succeed? If the first two owners of Beri were rather vague figures, Gosselin shows up as a man of substance with a wife, Emma, and five sons. We are on sure ground when we speak of him for his name is to be found as witness to important documents relating to St. Peter's, Exeter, and also in relation to Henry I and the Dukedom of Normandy. Two important acts which he carried out were, firstly, the redeeming of Beri from the monks of Gloucester, which was brought about by an exchange of land, and secondly his founding or perhaps refounding of the Abbey of St. Mary du Val in the diocese of Falaise, Normandy. There is in existence in Lefournier's 'Essai historique sur L'Abbaye de Notre Dame du Val' p.337, a transcript of the charter given in 1125 by Gosselin, with the consent of his wife, Emma, and their five sons. The surprising feature of this document is the large amount of land, churches, mills etc. which Gosselin had to give on both sides of the Channel. From this we can deduce that his father, Ralf, was, in the end, able to pass on to his sons a considerable inheritance. Of course, some of it may have been brought to Gosselin by his wife, since she is mentioned particularly as consenting to the gifts. In Devon the churches of Beri, Bradworthy and Clistwick were given. Beri remained in the hands of the Norman abbey until 1267 when it was exchanged with the Priory of Merton. Bradworthy was to be wrested from the grasp of St. Mary du Val at the end of the century by Lord William Brewer when he founded Torre Abbey.

We find from the document that Gosselin regarded his home as in Normandy, for he gives the abbey the "Campus de Cauville which is before our house" (nostram domum). This would appear to prove that the family had a footing still in Normandy, so did not look upon Beri yet as their permanent seat. It rather gives strength to the argument that the de la Pomerais had not as yet built themselves a home at Beri of any importance. They had, however, founded an Abbey, and in the 12th century that was very much a status symbol; to have an Abbey full of monks who would pray for you, your wife and family, forebears and successors for ever was much the same as taking out an insurance policy today. So by this act the family helped to establish its standing.

4. Henry de la Pomerai (I), (d.1166/7)

We shall presently see how in the Seymour family the name of Edward persisted through many generations; in the Pomeroy family there were no less than ten to bear the name of Henry. The first Baron of that name was the eldest son and heir of Gosselin and Emma. As his father was still alive between 1137 and 1141 he must have succeeded to his estates after this date. It was he who was destined to raise the standing of his family by moving very much in royal circles. He seems to have joined the court as early as 1121, for from that date he attests various charters at Westminster. Together with William, son of Odo, and Roger de Oyli, he held the office of constable in the household of King Henry I. At that time such an office was of considerable importance. He did even better than this, however, for he married no less a personage than Rohesia, a natural daughter of the King. She was, of course, a sister of Reginald, Earl of Cornwall, and in the Tregothnan Charter of (1145-56) he refers to his sister as Rohesia de Pomeria. There does not seem to be any evidence that Henry supported his brother-in-law in upholding Matilda's cause, neither does he appear to have been employed by Stephen. On the accession of King Henry II he was again to be found in royal service. He seems to have travelled about with the King and attests several important charters both in England and in Normandy. In 1158 he collaborated with the Chancellor, Becket, as judge in three counties.

Even from the few facts mentioned here it will be understood that the first Henry was but rarely seen in Devon and even less on his manor at Beri. He was much on the move, and it is interesting to note in passing how the pedigrees of both the Pomeroys and Seymours demonstrate that such a man was unlikely to found a family. The generations who spent their days mostly at Berry Pomeroy reared huge families. Henry I had only two sons, Henry (II) and Joscelin.

5. Henry (II) de la Pomerai
(c.1145-94)

He was the elder son of Henry de la Pomerai (1), and in spite of his mother's illegitimacy could claim to be a King's grandson. He was known as 'Henry the Son'. Some writers have stated that he and Henry (1) were one and the same person, but this would have made him between 70 and 80 in 1194 when he rebelled against King Richard I — a most unlikely time of life at which to begin such a hazardous undertaking. The reader can rest assured that he is well accounted for as a separate person. He married firstly Matilda de Viteri by whom he had one son, Henry (3), and secondly, Rohesia, daughter of Thomas Bardolf. He inherited 32 knight's fees in England but only one third of a fee in Normandy. In 1167 he is found with the Bishop of Bayeux where he in person confirmed all the rights given to the Abbey of St. Mary du Val by his grandfather and father. This included land and churches in England as well as in Normandy. The Liber Rubeus (635) shows that he still held the ancestral castle, the Chateau Ganne, from the King in 1172; and again in 1180 £30 was paid to a Robert de Pierrefitte for the custody of the castle of la Pomerai.

None of the recorded doings of this baron suggest that he ever came to reside at Berry, but his end is connected with the West Country for he fortified St. Michael's Mount against King Richard I, having first expelled the monks. He thus espoused the cause of Prince John, Count of Mortain and Earl of Cornwall. This was in

Quitclaim made by Ralf, Abbot of St. Mary de Valle, to Henry de Pomerai of lands in Bery (13th century)

1194. The various legends attached to his demise are told in the chapter on Folklore and need not be discussed again here. All that can be said for certain is that Henry was taken by surprise at the sudden return of King Richard I from captivity and abandoned the Mount; the story that he commited suicide by severing a vein is not feasible in the light of the charter discussed on p. 127, unless, of course, it reached him too late.

It will be noted that this baron did not follow up his father's example by living much at court and accepting royal appointments. The advantages gained by ties of blood with the royal family were quickly forgotten, it seems, and he ended his life by taking up arms against his king.

6. Henry de la Pomerai (III), (c. 1170-1207)

The third to bear the name of Henry seems to have been the only son and heir of Henry (2) de la Pomerai. He succeeded to his lands in 1194 encumbered by the debt of 700 marks owing to the Crown on account of his father's rebellion in the same year. Nine years later the debt was still unpaid, and the Exchequer demanded a payment of £66. 13s. 4d. annually until all was settled.

Henry (3) is the first of the family to transact any business in Devon. He helped Lord William Brewer in the founding of Torre Abbey by selling to him his manor of Bradworthy in 1198, with the exception of the church there, the chapel of Pankradeswike, molture from the mill and a ferling of land called Hidesburga — all of which was to be a part of the endowment of the new Abbey. This must have been rather humiliating to the family because the church was already a part of the endowment of the Norman Abbey of St. Mary du Val, which Henry's great grandfather had founded or refounded. In the Exchequer Cartulary of Torre Abbey (f.52/53) a charter from Henry de Pomerio is to be found confirming the gifts and also Hidesburga. In "Torre Abbey" I have described this ferling which can still be traced today with some certainty. St. Mary du Val Abbey, understanderbly, did not forego their possessions in Bradworthy without a struggle, and the legal wrangling which resulted is also described in "Torre Abbey". Henry on his side was short of money and no doubt pleased to sell Bradworthy. His name is not to be found among those who witnessed Torre Abbey's

Foundation Charter; this at first sight appears strange because as one of the leading landowners in this part of Devon one would have expected to see his name high on the list of signatories. I think the answer is to be found in the fact that, like his forbears, Henry (3) spent very little time in Devon. We know that in that year (1199), he was with King John at Andelys in August, when the King gave an important charter to the Knights Hospitallers. There is every reason to think that Henry spent much time in the entourage of the King, whether in England or Normandy.

In the last year of his life this baron did something at Berry — and it is the first of any such recorded acts — he enclosed with walls 100 acres of park. For this privilege he paid 10 marks in 1207. By this act it looks as though the family were just beginning to think that their manor of Berry was perhaps the best place to make their home.

Not a great deal is known of Henry (3). He married Alice de Vernon and by her had three sons, Henry (4), William and Geoffrey. During the whole of his life, through his father's treason, he owed much money to the Crown which he never succeeded in paying off.

7. Henry de la Pomerai (IV), (?-1221)

He was the eldest son and heir of Henry (3) and Alice Vernon. Dugdale (Baronage i,498), tells us that he had to pay a Fine of 600 marks for Livery of his lands. But his mother-in-law-to-be, Alice de Valletort, paid 400 marks of this, presumably upon the marriage between her daugther, Joan de Valletort, and Henry. This timely aid was perhaps regarded as part of her dowry. The impression one gets of this Baron is that he spent much more time in Devon than his forebears had done, for in 1215 he shared the Governorship of Exeter Castle with John de Erlegh, and he was later to be a Sheriff of Devon.

During the troubled days of the reign of King John he was at first loyal to the King but later fell away from him. For this his lands in Devon were seized. In September, 1216, however, a restitution was made, and he gave security for future loyalty. He also received Livery of the lands of Andrew Vitrei in Cornwall.

He was later to be found giving service to the King abroad, and was in his service at Poitou. The family can claim him as a Crusader, and in the year 1221 he was in Jerusalem where he entered into an agreement with brother Warren de Monte Acuto. He died in the same year, but it is not known where. Both Henry (4) and his father regarded themselves as blood relations of the King, and claimed membership of his 'private familia'. Such relatives each took an oath to report direct to the King anything which they heard to his detriment or harm. A legal battle in which he and Alan de Dunstanville were involved against one Baldwin Tyrell proves this point. The story is all to be found in Powley's "The House of de la Pomerai"; though of interest, it does not concern us here.

8. Henry de la Pomerai (V), (1211-1237?)

The fifth Henry de la Pomerai was the son and heir of Henry (4) and Joan de Valletort. He married Margaret de Vernon by whom he had one son, Henry (6). He was at first a ward of Ralf Trubleville. The debt on his lands in 1229/30 was £633. 18s. 10d. and two falcons, but his guardian enjoyed a moratorium until 1232. Henry came of age on July 20th, 1232, and after doing homage had Livery of his lands. It seems that as land owners the Pomeroy's influence was waning, for whereas in 1229/30 there is mention of 31 fees in Devon, yet by 1235/6 there were only 21 fees in his Barony. In the Somerset Mss., 135, we find that Henry (5) granted a charter to his borough of Brigg i.e. Bridgetown by Totnes. Once again this implies that the family was beginning to have a much closer connection with Berry than the first generations had. Very little of interest is known of this baron and he appears to have died young when only twenty-six or seven.

(9) Henry de la Pomerai (VI), (1236?1281)

At last we have a Pomeroy who must have lived at least for a part of his life on his manor of Berry, for we have record of an escapade wherein he broke into the park at Paignton of Walter Bronescombe, Bishop of Exeter. It is recorded in the Bishop's Register that he, thanks to Divine guidance, returned to his senses and promised to restock the park before next All Saints' Day. To make matters worse Henry seems at that time to have been under a sentence of excommunication, so from this we may not be wrong if we consider him something of a hothead in his youth. His promise to the Bishop dates from July 22nd, 1256.

This Baron was the only child of Henry (5) and Margaret de Vernon. Here was another case of wardship, for his father died young; but he seems to have been in his mother's custody in spite of the fact that a William Caperon is mentioned in 1242 as guardian of the de la Pomerai estates. In the year 1257, he was confirmed in possession of land at Up Otri (Devon Feet of Fines 611), so he must have come of age at about this time. He married Iseult de Bathonia; they had one son, Henry (7). The Welsh Wars claimed Henry in 1258, 1260, 1261, 1263 and 1264.

In 1267 an exchange of possession between the Abbey of St. Mary du Val and Merton Priory, Surrey, was arranged, and the church of Berry Pomeroy was thereafter the property of this Priory.

Meanwhile Henry had foolishly not observed the Provisions of Oxford and together with Richard and Terry de la Pomerai had joined Adam Gurdon and Brian de Gouiz against the King. He was apparently eventually pardoned in 1267.

Considerable estates in Cornwall should have been inherited by Henry through his grandmother, Joan de Valletort, and also by a cousin, Piers Corbet. A Fine of 1270, however, granted the estates elsewhere. So Henry and Piers put in their caveats in that year. This was to be the start of a long struggle for the Valletort estates which continued for several generations.

The Pomeroy estates continued to dwindle until there were only ten left in Devon. Tregony in Cornwall was retained, however. Henry granted fairs for Berry and Tregony and extended his father's charter to the tenants of Bridgetown.

Henry (6) was buried in the Church of the Dominican Friars at Exeter, but not before a strange occurrence in the Cathedral where his body was lying. The Friars entered the Cathedral choir, and against the will of the Dean and Chapter, seized the body, together with the wax, cloths and silk coverings, either offerings or the church's property, and took them away. They then buried the baron in their own church. One would much like to know why he was buried there and whether he had bequeathed his body to the Friars; and also whether he had made considerable gifts to them in his lifetime. What does emerge is the fact that he had identified himself with the people of Devon, having been at some time Governor of Exeter Castle and at another Sheriff of the County. He was the first of the family to have had a real footing in Devon and, so far as we know, the first to be buried there.

10. Henry de la Pomerai (VII) (1265-1305)

From the 5th to the 9th Henry the male descent was through only sons. Presently the senior line of the family was to fail to produce an heir as we shall see three generations further on. Henry was born and baptised on the family's manor of Tregony in Cornwall, thus proving that Berry was even by that time not looked upon as the principal seat of the Pomeroys. At the age of 16 he married Amicia de Caunville. He was under age when his father died and his father-in-law acted as guardian until he came of age in 1286. The following October (1287) he entered upon his inheritance. The family debt to the Crown still encumbered his estates. This amounted now to £300 which he was allowed to pay off in instalments. In connection with this debt a survey was made in 1292 of the estates of Beri, Stokleigh and Tregony. That concerning Berry is of the greatest interest and it is unfortunate that lack of space prevents a full account of it here. What interests us is the way in which the family's dwelling is described, for there is no mention whatever of a castle, simply a Hall (aula) with chambers, kitchen, grange, other buildings and gardens under the heading 'Demesne'. It was valued at £40. The manor court which would be held in this house brought in as perquisites another £40. So this was the manor house where the Pomeroys lived when they resided at Berry. The unpretentious scale of the premises could not by the greatest stretch of the imagination be considered as anything else but a small manor house — a hall-house which was so typical of the age we are considering. There is no reason to suppose that it stood anywhere else than on the site of the present manor house, beside the church, which is exactly the right place for it. I simply do not believe that the Pomeroys had a house on the site of the present castle at that time. The manor house today is obviously an ancient house surrounding a central courtyard and has already been described. Before leaving the subject of the Survey, however, it must be noticed that in 'Devon' Professor W.G. Hoskins (under Berry Pomeroy) states that the Survey of 1292 "shows only the usual type of mediaeval manor house on the site". This has been taken by some to imply that there is a map attached to the Survey which shows a manor house on the castle site. There is in fact nothing of the sort. Reichel (T.D.A. Vol.28) and Powley '(The House of Pomerai') have both dealt exhaustively with this Survey and neither mention any map of the castle site showing a manor house upon it. There is no evidence, therefore to show that any other site than that of the present manor house beside the church is being recorded in the Survey.

Meanwhile the legal battle for the Valletort estates continued unabated. In 1305 Henry and Piers Corbet (2) did receive a half each of manors of Brixham and Harberton, but the settlement of the Cornish estate of Trematon with its 60½ fees and the manor of Calstock seemed as far off as ever. Henry died in 1305, and by that time he held the manors of Berry with the rents at Bridgetown, half of Brixham and Harberton, some 33 fees in Devon and the manor of Tregony in Cornwall. He was thus in a comfortable state of affluence, in spite of the fact that his debt to the Crown was not yet paid off. It could have been he who began to build the castle we see today.

11. Henry de la Pomerai (VIII) (1291-1367)

He was the only son of Henry (7) and Amicia de Caunville. He was 14 at the time of his father's death and the ward of William Martyn. He came into possession of his lands by 1313 and married twice; (1) Joan de Moles and (2) Elizabeth, widow of Sir Roger Carminou.

After years of litigation and much cost, the settlement of the de Valletort estates with the Crown were at last achieved in 1338. Henry released the castle of Trematon and 60½ knights fees in Cornwall to the King, who granted him pardon of the debt to the Crown of £242 (how little his father had paid off!) and a pension of £40 p.a. until the King found him lands to the value of £30 p.a. He thus became a rich landowner and one of the most influential men in Devon. By 1338 he was therefore in a position to complete his castle, if indeed it had ever been begun; he must always be treated with respect as, perhaps, the most important of the long line of Pomeroys in that he did just that.

His first wife, Joan, must have been still living in 1348, for in that years she obtained from Pope Clement VII an indulgence to select confessors who were empowered to give plenary remission to them both in the hour of death. A British Museum document of 1351, which is a grant of a tenement within the east gate at Exeter to the Hospital of St John the Baptist, shows the seal of Henry (8) in red wax. "A shield of arms; a lion rampant with a bordure engrailed . . Above the shield and at each side a slipped holly or oak leaf. Within a carved gothic panel at eight points, ornamented along the inner edge with small trefoils, S'-Henrici-de-la Poumerai." Beaded border.

In spite of all the wealth and outward show of Henry's affluence there must, nevertheless, have been an element of disappointment in his life, for, unlike his ancestors, he was never summoned to Parliament. Why he was passed over we cannot tell; but although he had the qualifications of ancestry, and was a considerable owner of fees "in capite", yet he was never included in the Great Council of the realm. Now at this period it was becoming clear that those who were not summoned to Parliament were beginning to lose their status as barons. So although the lords of Berry lost no local prestige, yet from now on, although their tenure was still "By barony", yet the heads of the house were regarded as "knightly" rather than baronial.

12. Henry de la Pomerai (IX) (1305?-1373)

Sir Henry (9) was the eldest son of Henry (8) and Joan de Moles. The uncertain date of his birth, so Powley considers, could range from 1308-1319, but that is nonsense as his father died in 1305. It is not known whom he married, but he had a son, John, who died without issue, and two daughters. It was by Joan, the elder of these, that Berry was kept in the Pomeroy family, for her daughter, Joanna, married Sir Thomas Pomeroy, a collateral.

Henry (9) is one of the family about which little is known. He was a knight by 1340, and his chief claim to fame is that he fought in the battle of Crecy in 1346. So if it delights the reader to think that he rode forth from Berry arrayed in full armour for the fray we cannot deny such a possibility. He was in the retinue of John de Veer, Earl of Oxford, who was one of the commanders of the Black Prince's division. The Register of Bishop Brantyngham (Dec. 1373) shows that on Sir Henry's death he, with Thomas and William de la Pomerai and the vicar of Berry Pomeroy, Reginald de Horsyngtone, were to be responsible for the care of his goods, pending probate of his will.

13. John de la Pomerai
(c.1352-1416)

John at last broke the succession of nine generations of Henrys; but good fortune did not attend this change, for he died childless. He married Joan, daughter of Richard Merton; whether they had children who died in infancy we do not know, but there was no heir on John's death. He had done homage for his lands both in Devon and Cornwall by the end of 1374, so it is reasonable to assume that he was born about 1352. He would probably be knighted about the time that his homage was made. His arms as displayed on a herald's sketch of a seal on a document of 1376, and exhibited by Valentine Pomeroy of Sandridge, at a herald's visitation in 1620 was:— "A shield dependent from a helmet; a lion rampant within a bordure engrailed; a helmet, chaplet, surmounted by a lion sejant; the supporters, two Cornish choughs".

Sir John from the outset was much occupied in local affairs. In 1376 and again in 1377 he was one of eight commissioned to defend Devon against landings by the French, which at that time were considered probable. In 1379 and 1380 he was one of those appointed as commissioner of array, and it is most probable that he built the gatehouse and curtain wall at this time. All fit persons between 16 and 60 were to be equipped and the reluctant imprisoned. This was also the case in 1385. The year 1399 found Sir John as Sheriff of the county.

Although there is apparently no record of the licensing of a chapel at the castle, yet in 1391 he and his wife, Joan, were licensed by Bishop Brantygnham to have mass celebrated in any of their oratories in the Exeter diocese; and in 1410 they were licensed to choose confessors.

Sir John was much concerned with the succession to his estates should he die childless, and in 1387 he executed a resettlement of Berry so that in that case it should pass to the right heirs after his wife's death. Now under an entail made in 1328, John's cousin Edward, son of Thomas, who was the fifth son of Henry (8) should have been the male heir; but in 1404 Edward had shown himself content to receive from Sir John a conveyance of the manor of Tregony to himself and his heirs. Ten years later, however, in 1414, Edward was placed in an even better position, for, by a further agreement, he was to be the heir to all the estates after the death of Sir John's wife, Joan.

In 1414 Sir John did die childless as he had feared; but the Crown upheld the enfeoffment of 1387, and so his widow had Berry together with Stockleigh, Harberton and Brixham. The residue of these passed to Joanna, Sir John's neice, and to John Cole of Nitheway, his nephew. Now Joanna married thrice, her third husband being Sir Thomas de la Pomerai, who, the pedigree will show, came from a junior branch of the family. It was by this most judicious marriage that Berry was inherited by Sir Thomas on Sir John's death. So Edward was disappointed for the moment, but all came right for him in the end, because Sir Thomas and his wife died childless and everything came to him eventually. The year 1433 saw him definitely established at Berry.

14. Thomas de la Pomerai (I), (?-1428)

It can be safely asserted that Sir Thomas (1) was a colourful figure. Not many of the family have stood out in sharp relief on account of the things we know about them, but here is one who does — and he seems to have been at his worst something of a rogue and an adventurer, although his better side showed him as a King's knight — that is, one who had showed special service to the King, in this case Henry IV.

Now his marriage to Sir John's niece, Joanna, was a very coolly calculated affair, coming quickly after her uncle's settlement of Berry in 1387. Sir Thomas, being quite sure where she stood in the line of succession to the Berry estate, decided that he must marry the twice widowed Joanna at all costs, although it appears she was affianced to one William Amadas. They were married in haste in an aisle of the church of 'Byry pomeray' without the King's consent, by the vicar, Reginald Horsyngtone. No banns had been called and only J. Grey and Nicholas Kirkham were there as witnesses. The unfortunate vicar got into trouble over the affair with his diocesan, having to appear at Chudleigh before the Bishop's commissary in September 1388. He was ordered to abstain from fish every Friday for a year and refrain from saying mass until dispensed etc. Now Sir John's widow should have held Berry until her death in 1420, yet just before her death she gave it up to Sir Thomas and his wife, the right heir, and also to John Cole of Nitheway, Sir John's nephew. He was the son of Sir John's other sister, Margaret; but he immediately disappears from the scene. So after his wife's death in 1422 Sir Thomas enjoyed Berry and all the rest of the family estates until his death in 1428. There was one exception however, and that was the manor of Tregony in Cornwall. His tenant there, Edward, was on bad terms with him, as might have been expected. Matters were so strained by 1417 that Sir Thomas had to give a guarantee not to harm Edward.

With regard to public service, Sir Thomas was Sheriff of Devonshire in 1400 and in 1410, for Somerset and Dorset in 1404. He was chosen a knight of the shire for Devonshire in 1404, 1406, 1410 and 1413. In 1404 he was one of the M.P.s for the shire. In spite of all these honourable offices Sir Thomas was, it seems, ever in debt. In London he owed quite large sums of money to saddlers, vintners, drapers, tailors and armourers. In 1400 when Sheriff for Devon he fell into arrearage for £56. 13s. 4d. and was apparently imprisoned in the Flete. There exists a record of the warden there being ordered to free him.

Sir Thomas seems always to have played for high stakes and he usually won. He was certainly lucky to inherit Berry, but after his wife's death, when he might have remarried and founded a family, he did nothing of the kind, and the hated Edward at Tregony succeeded to everything. One would like to enquire how it was that he and his wife managed to get Sir John's widow to give up the castle to them. And what about John Cole of Nitheway? Did he, like the widow, conveniently die?

15. Edward Pomeray (I),
(c. 1404-1446)

A glance at the Pomeroy pedigree will show how Edward of Tregony, grandson of Henry (8), had a very good claim to the family estates on the death of Sir Thomas. By 1433 he was certainly in possession of Berry, for in that year enfeoffment and resettlement on himself, his wife, and heirs male were duly made. Parliament also accorded him full possession of the manor of Tregony. So what with Berry, Stockleigh and the Harberton and Brixham moieties Edward was an affluent member of Devon landholders. He took part in local affairs, being Sheriff in 1431, but he was never a knight. Note, too, that the family are now styling themselves as Pomeray and not de la Pomerai.

Edward married Margaret, the daughter of John Beville. There were two, possibly three, sons of this marriage. He died in 1446 and his heir received livery of Berry.

If we recognise two periods of building in the house we see today, then it is most probable that an extension to the first house would be made during Edward's regime. He certainly had the means, so far as we can see.

16. Henry Pomeray (X), (1423?-1487)

He was son and heir of Edward Pomeray and entered upon his possessions in 1446. It would appear that Berry and Tregony were his mother's property until her death in 1461/2. Henry married twice, firstly Alice, daughter of John Ralegh of Fardel Hall, and secondly Anne, widow of William Barrett, and daughter of Robert Cammel of Tittleford. By his first marriage there were five children.

These were the troublous days of the Wars of the Roses, and although Devon was outside the main stream of events, yet the countryside was disturbed, and Henry was amongst those constantly employed in arresting trouble makers and in the keeping of the peace both on land and sea. In spite of much activity in these local affairs Henry was never knighted or achieved distinction in any particular field of activity.

17. Richard Pomeray (1441?-1496)

Richard was the second son of Henry (10) and it would seem that his elder brother Sir Seintclere, died before his father; Richard was therefore the heir, and he entered upon his estates in 1487. He married Elizabeth Densell of Weare Giffard and by her he had four children. He proceeded to knighthood, being one of eleven K.B.s created by King Henry VII on the eve of the coronation of Elizabeth of York as Queen. He was sheriff of Devonshire in 1473 and 1492/3.

The rebuilding of the old Norman parish church of Berry Pomeroy is always attributed to Sir Richard, and his is the fine altar tomb on the north side of the Sanctuary. It was erected in memory of himself and his wife and is described in Prince's 'Worthies of Devon'. The church itself is described in an ensuing chapter so space will not be taken up here in further mention of it; but it must be the thing by which Sir Richard is best remembered.

His will, proved in October, 1496, contained a number of interesting bequests. He left 10 marks to the church at Berry and requested burial there. His son, Thomas, received £100 and half his jewels on his wife's death. 40/- was to be paid to the vicar of Berry for "thithes overlooked". Each domestic was to have a year's wages. A silver gilt cup went to the Friars Preachers of Exeter to pray for his soul, whilst 5 marks was given to the Cathedral. There was 5 marks for the abbot of Tavistock and another 5 for the convent. The abbots of Torre and Buckfast each received 40/-. Edward, his son, had a little chain of gold and Thomas a larger one. After making several other smaller bequests Sir Richard left the residue to his widow. In 1497 she received her third of the honour and castle of Berry.

Elizabeth's third share is the most precious of the documents which describe the castle — and over the years they are very few. It consisted of "a great chamber beyond the castle gate with the cellar on the left of the gate, with two chambers beyond and belonging to the said great chamber, a kitchen, a larderhouse and a chamber beyond the kitchen; her third of the capital messuage of the manor of Bury Pomery, a pantry, a buttery and all chambers beyond and under the said pantry and buttery up to the chamber there called the Stuerdischambre with a moiety of the Bakehouse, Bruhouse, Kechyn, and Lardehouse, and a stable for horses with a loft built over it, a barne called Barle Barne and a house called Kyrtelsbarn"; there follow names of five fields and two gardens in the barton. There is also mention of a third of the park of Beri with its deer. The careful description of the rooms allotted to her is considered in the chapter on the castle itself. Elizabeth enjoyed all this until 1503, for she was dead by March of that year.

Richard Pomeray's will shows that he was very much a son of the Church. When one remembers that he rebuilt the church of Berry, leaving money to it and the vicar, in case he had not paid all the tithe he should have done, and that he also left more money to several religious houses, the conclusion is that he was of a pious turn of mind. This being so it is more than probable that he ordered the painting of the fresco in the gatehouse with its religious subject, for it is said to date from this period. If this is the case, then in the panel containing the head and shoulders of a man and his wife, with a castle tower in the background, it is more than likely that we actually have likenesses of Richard and his lady, Elizabeth Densell.

18. Edward Pomeray (II) (1478-1538)

The second Edward entered into his estates in 1501, being the eldest son of Richard Pomeray and his wife, Elizabeth Densell. He received knighthood on the 18th February, 1503/4 on the occasion of King Henry VII's son, Henry, Duke of York, being created Prince of Wales. Sir Edward married Joan, daughter of Sir John Sapcotes by whom he had six children.

In 1501 he became a 'knight of the body' and a member of the household of King Henry VII. Later, in 1520, he was listed among those to attend King Henry VIII at the Field of the Cloth of Gold. So it will be seen that in the early part of his life he was much at Court.

One of the few things which we know about him with regard to local affairs concerned the town of Totnes where he was in dispute with the Mayor and Corporation. This dispute was taken to arbitration and the award was so tactful as to be beyond belief. Both sides were ordered to feast each other annually. "The said Sir Edward shall give the maiour and his brethren a buck of this season to be eton at Totneys upon Wenysday next before the feast of the Nativitie of our Blessed Lady next ensuying the date hereof or afore ... the same Sir Edward be at the etyng of the same bucke in goodly manner ... the said maiour and his brethren shall paye for the wyne which shall be dronk at the etyng of the same bucke".

Sir Edward is said to have died on October 21st, 1538, his wife surviving him.

19. Thomas Pomerey (II) (1503-1566/7)

Thomas (2) was the eldest son of Sir Edward (2) and Joan Sapcotes. He came into his possessions in 1539 and married Joan, eldest daughter of Piers Edgcumbe.

He seems to have been a restless man who was always buying and selling land. Old writers all refer to him as squandering his inheritance. On November 17th, 1548, was signed the fatal document whereby he sold Berry Pomeroy, Bridgetown Pomeroy, Hurberton and Herberton to the Lord Protector, the Duke of Somerset, for £4000. It has been quite wrongly stated that he forfeited the castle and lands because he fought on the side of the rebels in the Western Rebellion. That, however, did not take place until the ensuing year, so it is quite clear that it had nothing whatever to do with the sale. Why ever did he part with his fine castle which his family had owned for nineteen generations? The most likely conclusion is that he was in debt and needed the money. Recent consideration of the main buildings seem to point to the fact that the Pomeroys had enlarged the house in the 15th century and perhaps again even later. But Sir Thomas's restless temperament may have desired an entirely new mansion built on a less confined space than the clifftop castle. That may have been why he sold the manors of Sandridge, Brixham and Stockleigh Pomeroy in 1544/6. With the money obtained and the £4000 which the Duke paid for Berry he would have been in a position to build a grand mansion somewhere. Yet he and his brother, Hugh, seem in the meantime to have invested in Chantry lands.

Fortune turned her wheel and no house was begun in 1549, for Sir Thomas made the mistake of his life by throwing in his lot with the rebels in the Western Rebellion of Whitsuntide that year. At Clyst, Sir Thomas, with a trumpeter and drummer, hid himself in a furze brake to the rear of Lord Russell's army. He then sounded the alarm which so frightened the army that they thought they had been ambushed and retreated hurriedly, suffering heavy losses. But the army recovered and routed the rebels. Sir Thomas was taken prisoner and with nine other traitors was marched to London. Four of them were hanged, drawn and quartered, but Sir Thomas was one of five to be reprieved from this horrible end. He managed to retain his knighthood into the bargain. Writers have assumed that a heavy fine was paid to the Crown, yet no record of any such thing has come to light. Between 1566 and 1567 he died, but where had he lived for sixteen years or so? Many say at Sandridge, yet he had sold this in 1544. Certainly this estate came back to the family later, as his grandson, Valentine, was referred to as "of Sandridge". Sir Thomas's son, another Thomas, lived at Beenleigh, near Harbertonford. Was it here that the ageing Sir Thomas ended his days? I was certainly told so on one occasion when I visited Beenleigh, but actual proof seems wanting at the moment.

So in 1548 ended a connection of over four centuries between the Pomeroys and the castle. It will have been seen from the foregoing short accounts of each generation that the first were barons and considered as "of the King's household". Later they were regarded as "chivalers" or knights, but their prestige in the county never suffered because of this downgrading. They constantly held high office in Devon. Now the legendary Pomeroys who come down to us in folklore are quite a different breed, and they are considered in the chapter on the castle's folklore. Apart from the second Sir Henry, whose end may have been melodramatic, the reader will have seen that members of this family never did anything spectacular, nor did they enjoy high office in the country. They were respected country gentry, and their lives are particularly well accounted for in the county's records to which there is no difficulty in gaining access. But the strange and fantastic stories which surround the Pomeroys in folklore are as fascinating as the truth is unromantic.

Pedigrees
Pomeroy   p. 172-3
Seymour   p. 174

Edward Seymour, Earl of Hertford, 1st Duke of Somerset and Lord Protector, who purchased Berry Pomeroy in 1548

CHAPTER 3

BERRY UNDER THE SEYMOURS
(1548 to the present day)

Like the Pomeroys the Seymours derived from an ancient Norman family. The writer of the 'Annals' traces them back through the 8th century to St. Maur-sur-Loire, from which village they took their name. Stories about the family going even further back the author treats as legendary. Documentary evidence comes to our aid in 1009 with the marriage of a Goscelin de Saint Maur with Auremburge. His second son Guillaume had a son named Wido who accompanied the Conqueror to England. His name appears on the list in both Holinshed's and Stow's Chronicles of those who actually fought at Hastings. Like the Pomeroys the St. Maurs lived as country gentry, holding local office in the Provinces. In 1240 a Sir William St. Maur held Penhow Castle in Monmouthshire. In the 15th century the name became Seymour and by the mid century the family were seated at Wolfhall in Wiltshire. Three generations of Sir Johns bring us to the father of both Jane Seymour and the Lord Protector. On their mother's side they were descended from John of Gaunt, so Henry the VIII was more than wise when he married Jane, for the marriage rather nipped in the bud any pretensions which this by now powerful family may have had to the Tudors' insecure throne.

King Edward VI
and his uncle the Lord Protector

1. Sir Edward Seymour (I), later Duke of Somerset, Earl of Hertford, Viscount Beauchamp and Baron Seymour of Hache, (c. 1506-1552)

What did the tenants at Berry Pomeroy and Bridgetown think when they learnt that Sir Thomas Pomerey had sold his birthright? After an association of well over 450 years the old Catholic family were in 1548 superseded by the strongly Protestant Seymours. At that moment the Duke was Lord Protector of the Realm and the most powerful man in the land — the uncle and guardian of the boy King, Edward VI. There can be little doubt that the new family, whose estates lay far away from Devon, would at first be resented, for they were strangers in this part of the country. One notices that an attempt to call the manor Berry Seymour did not succeed, and the old name persisted. At about this time the memory of the Pomeroys would grow fabulous in the minds of the peasantry round about. The old days soon became the good old days to them, and the bad things were forgotten. Then in a very short time was not their new landlord disgraced and executed? So what sort of people were these Seymours?

This is perhaps not the place to write at length about the life of the Lord Protector, but since he was the first Seymour owner of the castle he is of great importance to those who are interested in its history. He was born about 1506, and as a young man was a friend of King Henry VIII, having been a page at Court from an early age. He and the King had a common interest in the sport of tilting. On the occasion of the marriage of his sister, Jane, to the King he was created Viscount Beauchamp of Hache in Somerset. In 1536 he became Earl of Hertford, and on the death of the King in 1547 King Edward VI made him High Steward of England, Treasurer of the Exchequer, Earl Marshall of England, Baron Seymour of Hache and Duke of Somerset. In the patent conferring the Barony it was expressly stated that one reason for conferring it was that the name of Seymour should not fall into oblivion, sunk in the titles which he was to bear; for to that name the King expressed a great attachment, on account of its having been borne by his most beloved mother, Queen Jane of England.

In 1548, the Duke concluded negotiations begun in 1547 for the purchase of Berry Pomeroy and Bridgetown, among other estates, from Sir Thomas Pomerey. Very shortly he was to be brought down by the jealousy of his enemies, and after a summary trial was executed on Tower Hill in 1552, his young nephew, King Edward VI, making no effort to save him. This was all to the great grief of the common people who were devoted to him, even to dipping their handkerchiefs in his blood after the execution. This, then, was the first of the new family to own the castle.

2. Sir Edward Seymour (II)
(c. 1529-1593) known as Lord Seymour

He was the second son of the Lord Protector by his first marriage. His second marriage was disastrous for the two brothers of the first marriage, for their father cut them off from succeeding him. It was in point of fact to be another six generations before the Dukedom of Somerset returned to the senior line. Sir John Seymour, the elder brother, seems to have been on bad terms with his father who completely disinherited him. He died, unmarried, in 1552. Sir Edward, however, in spite of the second marriage, seems to have got on well with his father, and when only 18 accompanied him on the Scottish Campaign in 1547. Here he distinguished himself at the Battle of Musselburgh by rallying scattered cavalry. For this gallantry he received a knighthood. He seems to have been constantly in attendance upon his father at Hampton Court with King Edward VI. So when his father was disgraced and sent to the Tower it was not surprising that Sir Edward was also imprisoned there. It was not until some months after his father's execution that he was eventually released. His elder brother died in 1552, and by an Act of March 27th of that year he inherited the Maiden Bradley estate in Wiltshire. This Act did not restore to him his father's estates, however. But in the same year the Patent Rolls (1547-1553) record that Sir Edward Seymour, son of Edward, late Duke of Somerset, received in consideration of the sale of lands in Somerset, Gloucester and Wiltshire "grant . . . of the . . . manors of Bury Pomerye, Devon, late of Edward, duke of Somerset etc., and formerly of Thomas Pomerey, knight, and the lands called Halwood' (there follows a list of some twenty fields), 'the advowsons of Bury Pomery, Devon, and the rectory of Ellyngton, Hunts; and all other lands in Bury, Burye Pomerye, Bridgetowne Pomerey, Iplepen, Netherton, Langcombe and Afton, Devon, late of the said duke and Thomas Pomerye, knight . . .

"To hold the said premises in the said county of Devon to the said Edward Seymour, knight, and his heirs and assigns of the King in chief by the service of a fortieth part of a knight's fee, etc."

So Lord Seymour did not inherit Berry Pomeroy from his father, as some writers have erroneously stated, but received both it and Bridgetown back from the Crown in consideration of the sale of lands in Somerset, Gloucestershire and Wiltshire. How far this was a bad bargain we cannot tell, but it seems that he was fortunate in being able to establish himself as a man of property so quickly after his father's disgrace. By this time his complete innocence of the charges brought against him was no doubt established. Although his father purchased Berry in 1548 it is doubtful if he ever saw it, but Sir Edward made it his chief seat until his death in 1593, soon enlarging it in a magnificent style.

Now in the same year that Sir Edward bought back Berry Pomeroy the delicate King Edward VI died and his sister Mary — a Catholic — ascended the throne. So it behoved the Seymours, who had for so long identified themselves with the Protestant cause, to tread warily. Sir Edward retired into private life and contrived not to get embroiled in the religious upheavals of the times. In 1558, when Queen Elizabeth I succeeded, he received 'pardon' from her — for no offence that we know of, except that his father's disgrace would still place the family under a cloud from an official point of view. Two years later the Queen, always short of cash, borrowed £100 from Sir Edward, to be repaid before Christmas, 1563. As the writer of the 'Annals of the Seymours' wryly comments, "In return she gave him a promissory note which has not yet been redeemed".

In 1562 Sir Edward married Jane Walsh, whose father was Sergeant-at-Law and later one of the Justices of Common Pleas. The living of Berry Pomeroy at the Dissolution of the Monasteries had come into the hands of King Henry VIII. By this time Sir Edward's father-in-law had procured it and presented it to his son-in-law.* He appears now to have settled down, like the Pomeroys before him, to administering his estate. The threat of trouble with Spain was soon

---

*The living must have got out of his hands again for it was included in the transaction of 1553 mentioned above.

to fill men's minds, and for anyone living near the Channel coast the threat of invasion was ever present. In 1580 Sir Edward bought Torre Abbey from Sir Hugh Pollard. I think that a possible reason for this was to prevent its falling into Catholic hands. Although some Catholics were extremely steady in their loyalty to Queen Elizabeth, yet others were much hoping for a Spanish invasion. The wisdom of Sir Edward's purchase was to be seen when in 1588 the Spanish galleon, the "Nuestra Senora del Rosario", was captured and brought into Torbay. The crew of 397 were brought ashore and Sir Edward was able to house them in the old tithe barn at Torre Abbey until other accommodation was found.

In 1583 Sir Edward was made Sheriff for Devonshire; he also held positions as Deputy Lieutenant and Justice of the Peace. In 1584 we find a return made by him and Sir John Gilberte of all the demi-lances and light horse for the hundreds of Devon, also an Instrument of Association for the county signed by himself, Sir John Gilberte and Sir Francis Drake. In 1588, when the Armada threat increased, Sir Edward was in command of a body of troops.

We read that in 1589, when a captured Spanish galleon was brought into Dartmouth he housed the prisoners at his "house" at Berry Pomeroy until the ship was cleared. On board were found 85 pipes of wine, but in such bad condition that only 67 pipes from the best of it could be made. This, Gilberte and Cary reported to the Council, they had bestowed upon Sir Edward in gratitude for his encumbering his house with prisoners. A sour reward, it appears!

The remainder of his life Sir Edward employed upon his estates here and in Wiltshire. His business acumen aided him in establishing himself as a considerable landowner. He seems to shine through the pages of history as an indomitable character, who, given more advantageous circumstances politically, might have risen to hold high office as his father did before him.

3. Sir Edward Seymour (III) (c. 1563-1613). First Baronet

It would appear that Edward, the son and heir of Lord Seymour, was born at the castle in 1562/3, for at the tender age of two or three he was betrothed to Elizabeth Champernowne of Dartington Hall. She was the daughter of Arthur Champernowne, so the two families and near neighbours must have been on very friendly terms. The marriage took place ten years later. In those days there was good reason for such early betrothals, for if the father of a family were to die, then his child, if not of age, would have a guardian who might dictate just whom his ward was to marry. Some guardians were quite unscrupulous and married their wards to the highest bidder. But when once a child was betrothed there was no risk of such an occurrence.

Edward developed quickly, for at 20 he was appointed Deputy Vice-Admiral for the county of Devon, and later became Sheriff. In 1586 we find him Vice Admiral for Cornwall. These early appointments speak much for the ability which he evidently showed. In 1593 his father died and he received a special licence under the Great Seal in the following year to enter into all his estates which, thanks to his father's zeal, were now considerable. From the evidence of recent excavation we can be sure that it was he and his father who began the ambitious rebuilding and enlarging of the castle. Certainly one would gather that from a material point of view he was affluent enough to have done so. Prince tells us that the cost was some £20,000—a vast sum in those days.

During the final decade of the 16th century there was renewed anxiety as to the threat of a Spanish invasion. The security of the coast of South Devon was in the hands of George Cary of Cockington and Sir Edward. They received orders from the Privy Council as to the best means of appointing and disposing of the bands and companies of trained and untrained men in their command. The defence of Dartmouth was in the hands of Sir John Gilberte of Greenway. When the latter became indisposed Sir Edward took his place; as a result he received a commission as Colonel from the Lord Lieutenant on September 5th, 1595. His regiment consisted of 1600 able men, but only 916 had arms of any kind. Later he and Cary and Gilberte had permission to requisition arms. We are told in the "Annals of the Seymours" that as the clergy always had a secret store of weapons in their houses, the greater part of the men were soon armed! During the whole of 1598 the Colonel was engaged in levying troops for service in Ireland; in the end they were never required. Although in this year the invasion scare was at its height, the Colonel sold Torre Abbey to Sir John Ridgeway who was already lord of the manor of Tormohun and a Protestant, so that corner of the bay could be considered in safe hands. The invasion, of course, never came and by 1599 the regiments were gradually disbanded. It should be noted in passing that money from the sale of Torre Abbey no doubt helped in the cost of enlarging the castle.

On the accession of King James I in 1603 Colonel Seymour received a royal pardon just as his father had done from Queen Elizabeth. One can only suppose that his grandfather's disgrace meant that the family was still regarded as attainted from a strictly legal point of view. In 1601 he was chosen to serve in Parliament as knight of the shire for Devon, and again from 1604-1611. He was twice Sheriff of Devon, and with the prestige gathered from his now magnificent seat at Berry, it was not surprising that he was created a Baronet in 1611. In spite of the fact that he was the grandson of a Duke this was a dignity which was well merited. The recipient of such an honour, nevertheless, had to pay dearly for it in an indirect way. The King needed money, and it looks as though in this case £1,095 changed hands (Annals p.267).

Sir Edward died at the castle on April 11th, 1613, and was buried in the parish church with due solemnity. The sermon was preached by Barnaby Potter, later Bishop of Carlisle. In due course a large monument in the Corinthian style was erected to his memory in the north chapel of the church where it still is—and in excellent condition, too. It consists of the recumbent figures of himself, his wife and his father. Below are the figures of his five sons and four daughters. (But whoever is the delightful little creature seated on his right hand side?) The monument implies that this was a man of wealth and influence. He re-established the fortunes and standing of the older branch of the family, which, through no fault of his own, were wrested from his unfortunate grandfather, the Lord Protector. Sir Edward seems to have been a model officer and to have carried out all his military duties punctiliously. His public offices in the county and in Parliament were also discharged creditably.

In the "Annals" there are some interesting letters between him and Lord Bath with respect to military operations. Some were actually written from Berry Pomeroy Castle. It is as a soldier that Sir Edward will be remembered, and for some twenty years of his life he was always referred to as Colonel Seymour.

4. Sir Edward Seymour (IV) (1585-1659). Second Baronet

It is most probable that the second baronet was born at Berry Pomeroy, but little is known of his early years. He received knighthood at the hands of King James I at Greenwich on May 22nd, 1603, at the age of eighteen. His father had done much to make the name of Seymour respected in Devon: he had married from a local family and most probably brought to fruition the costly enlargement of his castle. By the time that the second baronet succeeded in the year 1613 he would inherit no mean birthright. The fact that he was taken for granted locally as a man of ability is proved by his having been appointed Governor of Dartmouth. The next thirty years was to see the castle at the height of its prosperity. Judging from Prince's description of the new wing on the northwest side of the buildings a splendid home had been brought into being; at that time there must have been few houses in Devon to rival it.

Sir Edward married Dorothy Killegrew and by her raised a family of six sons and five daughters. In 1617 he became Deputy Lieutenant of the County, and in 1620 was given command of a regiment raised in South Devon. From 1622 onwards he became involved in shipping, for he had become an officer of the Admiralty with powers over the Devon coast. We read in the "Annals" of a complaint from one Robert Dure of St. Malo who petitioned the Council on behalf of the merchants of that town, to call Sir Edward Seymour, James Bagg and Thomas Harding, all Admiralty Officers, to answer a charge of taking a ship of theirs and bringing it into Plymouth where they refused to take it in charge, but aided and abetted their captors in embezzling and selling the goods therein, maltreating the master and mariners, and had finally sold the vessel for a very small sum. No notice seems to have been taken of this complaint (Annals p.271).

In 1625 Sir Edward served as M.P. for Hillington and twice for Totnes. But his seafaring exploits absorbed much of his time and energy. These must have been most lucrative, for he kept two ships at Dartmouth, one of which was described as "warlike". On April 28th, 1626, he brought into that port an Irish barque; on searching for the prize what should they find stowed away in her but a Catholic priest from Douay! In the same year his "warship" the

"Reformation of Dartmouth" had captured the "Joshua". The State Papers Domestic of Charles I show Sir John Eliot complaining to the Council that as Vice-Admiral of the County he was entitled to half the value of ships taken. The reward from the "Joshua" was £1,000, but the Duke of Buckingham had given it all to Sir Edward. Providing that his ships in their Admiralty capacity policed the Channel, King Charles I does not seem to have minded what their owners did in their own interests. So Sir Edward went on his way, quite openly filling his coffers and carrying on the building project at the castle. Prince in his account of it waxes lyrical. I always delight in his statement that for a servant but to open all the casements of the many apartments and then to close them again in the afternoon was "a good day's work". The Inventory of 1688 indicates over 50 rooms. There is little doubt that the Seymours lived here in style.

Bad times were ahead, however, for the Civil War greatly impoverished the family. Sir Edward threw in his lot with his Sovereign and immediately became embroiled with the Parliamentarians. The High Sheriff had summoned the people to muster at Modbury in the King's name. Sir Edward and his son raised men, and on their way to Modbury were surprised by a party of Parliamentarians who took them prisoner and dispatched them to London. After a few weeks Sir Edward gained his release through an exchange of prisoners. On his return he found that a party of enemy horse had visited the castle, seizing goods to the value of £89 12s. 6d. in spite of resistance by his retainers.

Being now too advanced in age to be of much use in the field he stayed quietly at Berry Pomeroy, leaving the active fighting to his sons. Nevertheless he was not left alone to end his days in peace, for Cromwell sequestrated all his Devonshire estates on account of his having raised troops at Modbury. All rents were received by the Parliament, but Sir Edward was not turned out of his castle. The fact that he lived on there until his death in 1659 confutes the legend that one side of the building was battered to bits by a canonade from the hill opposite. I have pointed out elsewhere that he certainly did not live on for over ten years in a ruin. Besides all that, his son, after many vicissitudes, succeeded him there.

It is unfortunate that he did not live long enough to see the Restoration of 1660, for he died on October 5th of the preceding year. He was buried at Berry Pomeroy. There is no grandiose memorial to him in the church, it being doubtful if the family could have afforded one at that time. His chief memorial must have been the splendid house which he continued to build until the outbreak of hostilities. But he never completed it. The "Annals" comment that he died "very much lamented, having by an obliging temper attracted the love of his country; and by a prudent management gained the character of a person of honour, conduct and experience". In spite of these eulogies I see him as a seadog of the same calibre as Drake and Raleigh—a smuggler, if you will. As Governor of the port of Dartmouth he had everything on his side. He would land his prizes on the river above Stoke Gabriel at Fleet Mill Creek, where in those days there would be a private jetty. This was the landing place for the castle. Here his packponies awaited the prizes, and conveyed them from the creek up the steep single track lane—still quite unchanged from that day to this. At Berry Pomeroy there was ample stowage space on the ground floor of the facade we still see. Perhaps that is why it does not look as though it was ever meant to be lived in.

5. Sir Edward Seymour (V) (1610-1688). Third Baronet

The third baronet was the last of the family to reside at Berry Pomeroy. By his wife, Anne Portman, he had a family of five sons and one daughter. It is most probable that all were born at the castle. A portrait of Anne at Knoyle is still in existence and included here. Whilst in his twenties his father made over his Maiden Bradley estate in Wiltshire to him. He served in the two final Parliaments of King Charles I as a knight of the shire. From the very outset of the Civil War he was active on the King's behalf, and very dearly did he pay for it. In July of 1642 he was empowered to raise a regiment of 12,000 men, being given a commission as Colonel. It has already been told how in that very same year he and his father were surprised and taken prisoners whilst on their way to a muster of Royalists at Modbury. Nevertheless he was soon at liberty again, and just whether he escaped from captivity or was exchanged for another prisoner we do not know. Be that as it may, in April, 1643, he received a second commission to raise 1,500 foot, and this Regiment operated in the north of Cornwall and in South Devon. In September of that year Prince Maurice ordered him to take the town and castle of Dartmouth, but his force was insufficient. The Prince therefore joined him with a part of his army and the town was taken, though with difficulty. The Colonel was then placed in command as Governor of Dartmouth.

In the winter of that year he undertook special journeys for the King. He met the King at Oxford, going to Cornwall via Tavistock and returning the same way. The object of the journeys were kept secret and no correspondence on the subject survives. Letters between the Colonel and the King, Prince Maurice, Sir R. Grenville and others are preserved and are of decided interest to all who study the progress of the war in South Devon. In 1644 the Colonel was given permission to erect a powder mill at Totnes which was to supply his large magazine at Dartmouth. Plymouth was besieged in April of this year by the King's forces and he was asked to send reinforcements, arms and ammunition there. He was also authorised to appoint watches at the beacon fires and to distribute horsemen and musketeers at convenient places along the coast between Teignmouth and Plymouth.

By midsummer things began to go badly for the Royalist cause in the West. Weymouth was captured and the siege of Plymouth still continued. The news of the defeat at Marston Moor was disastrous to the Royalists everywhere. Dartmouth had finally to surrender to the Parliament and the Colonel was harshly treated on account of the conspicuous part he had played in the defence of the South-West. His estate at Maiden Bradley was seized, also the Berry Pomeroy estate which his father had made over to him; as no tenant was ever put in possession his father was allowed to live on at the castle. Eventually the Colonel was able to bargain for the Maiden Bradley estate for the sum of £1,200. His treatment, nevertheless, was severe and he was imprisoned in Exeter for some years, most unjustly it appears. When finally he was set free in 1655 he had to enter into an Agreement to surrender himself to General Desborough or Sir John Copplestone whenever required. It is clear that Cromwell regarded him with the greatest suspicion and concerned deeply in Royalist plots, which no doubt he was! In spite of their impoverished state both father and son managed to send considerable sums of money to King Charles II. For this purpose the Colonel sold Totnes Castle and all family property in Totnes. In 1658 it is believed he actually managed to get across to France to visit the King and take him £1,000—a truly risky business. At this period the old castle must have sheltered many who were deeply concerned in Royalist plots.

The Colonel succeeded to the baronetcy on his father's death in 1659. His years of harassment were then practically at an end. When in 1660 the Restoration took place, Sir Edward's name leads all the rest in the signatures attached to "the declaration of the Gentrie of the King's party in the County of Devon".

His life now became more peaceful, and, like his forebears, he took his part in public life. He was soon Deputy Lieutenant of the county and later Vice-Admiral. For many years he represented Totnes in Parliament. Amongst his papers was a settlement of 1664 which proves that the castle was intact at that time and had never been destroyed by Cromwell's cannons as folklore has it. There is also mention of a mansion in the Park of Berry Pomeroy, a capital house and barton. The site of this mansion is discussed in the chapter concerning the Park.

In 1688, the final year of his life, Sir Edward was chosen a member for the city of Exeter. He was at this time active in association with those who were anxious to invite William of Orange to take the Crown. On his arrival at Brixham he is said to have welcomed the Prince at Berry Pomeroy, but I have so far not been able to confirm for certain that the Prince really did visit the castle. If he did this would be the very last occasion when any pomp and ceremony took place there.

Sir Edward was buried at Berry Pomeroy. The writer of the "Annals" comments: "He appears to have been looked upon as a soldier of great courage and ability, and when in Parliament as a statesman of the steadiest principles, esteemed by all for his honour and integrity". He was a loyal subject of the Stuart cause until the actions of James II could no longer be reconciled with the Constitution. Then he and his whole family embraced the cause of the Prince of Orange.

This account of the third baronet would not be complete without mention of his wife. She was active in attempting to get her husband set free when he was so long imprisoned in the Marshalsea at Exeter. She took a letter from him herself to London to be presented to the Council of State. Sir Edward wrote: "For if not granted (his request) I intend to send my wife—and I pray advise the Council of State from me, in relation to their own quiet, let them grant my request rather than be punished with her importunity." Lady Anne survived her husband, dying in 1692. Among her bequests were silver dishes, spoons and looking-glasses given to her by the King of Spain, a sword given to her husband by Charles II and many other such articles which she desired might remain in the Seymour family for ever. "One of them" writes the 11th Duke of Somerset, "probably on account of its small value, has remained longer than she had reason to expect, and that is a buff coat which she says was her husband's." We are told in the "Annals" that it is still preserved as one of the antiquities of Berry Pomeroy. But it is now eighty years since the publication of that book and the present Duke of Somerset writes, "There is no coat at Maiden Bradley belonging to the third Baronet; in fact the only personal relic from Berry is the saddle and accoutrements belonging to the third Baronet, said to be the saddle which he used when going to welcome William of Orange at Torbay. It was found buried in a box in the castle, and is in a very good state of preservation. There is no silver, sadly, and we have no portraits of the Berry Castle Baronets . . ."

A valuable survival is an Inventory of the castle made upon the baronet's death in 1688, December 10th. The following rooms are mentioned: "Closet or study, my ladyes chamber, my ladyes closett, my ladyes dressing room, great parlour, passage, hall, buttery, sellar, deary, wash-house, brewhouse, syderhouse, lodge, ffore chamber, lodge in the middle chamber, groomes chamber, toolehouse, chamber over, work house, kitching, lawde and pantry, little parlour, parlour chamber, staire chamber, little hall, hall chamber, blew chamber, deary chamber, little deary chamber, woll chamber, mault chamber, chamber over malthouse, two rooms above the maulthouse, two roomes over the brew house, Mr. Carter's chamber, next room to Mr. Carter's chamber, roome next to my ladyes chamber, servants chambers". Goods and chattels were valued at £414. 9s. 6d. Corn in the barns and granary, wheat in the ground, implements, horses, cattle and sheep made up a grand total of £918. 12s. 6d.

The Inventory proves that Sir Edward was not living in a house which was partly in ruins owing to bombardment by the Roundheads. If such an attack ever took place, then he had rebuilt. The house contained over 40 rooms; these with an unspecified number of servants' chambers would bring the total to around fifty.

This brief sketch of the life of the third Baronet concludes with four letters happily preserved for us among the Somerset Papers at

Trowbridge. Their droll and witty style will soon endear him to the reader. One can but hope that they entertained Lady Anne as she awaited her husband's return to Berry. Ned is, of course, the eldest son, and it seems that at this period he and his father were at loggerheads. Both men were Members of Parliament and it seems that they had quarrelled over money matters. The final letter from a mutual friend, Will Jesson, shows how anxious he was to bring about a reconciliation.

Box 53

London, March 22nd, 1661

My Dear Heart

I writt you last and dyrected my letter to Salisbury. I hope this may find you at Berry, from whence the sooner I hear from you the speedier I shall be wth you. There is noe kindness iustice(?) to be hoped for from my most undutifulle sonn. This afternoon I have perswaded Sr Hugh Pollarde to goe to Sir Wm Wal^r & my sonn and treat wth them, to moderate their rigorous & uniust dealing wth me. In fine I fear ther is no good to be expected from them, the more my misfortune, to finde my erro^r when to late to repaye it. Ther was on Wensday last A sharp contest in the House of Peers concerning a Proviso to be added in the Bill for Uniformity, wch was so that all the tender consciences should, if they pleasd be free from being compelld to use either the Surplice, or Cross in Baptisme. It was mainly opposed by divers. Though countenanced & abetted by the Chancellor & fower of the Bishopps. Thursday in the afternoon my Ld Duke of Albemarle was again visited wth A sharpe fitt of an Ague after it had left him A weeke. This day my Ld Marlborough began his voyage for the east Indyse. Catell wth his luggage goes Aboard this day for Devon bound. S^r ffrances Beddingfeild had a letter wch gave an Account of my sons Hugh's having been at his house, in his way to Sevill in Spaine, but is now againe on his way returne for Lisbone, & intends to returne wth the Queene. Harry is very well at Garnsey. I received an assurance from his owne hand. My Lady Portman ar very well so was my sonn John. My Lady Crookes incessant importunityes forced by her urging occasions gives me no rest by day & others any by night. So that you may conclude this letter came from A member of Bedlam. My hearty service to all my neighbours & friends especially Will Bogan and his Lady & Mr. Kelland & Mrs. Maynard Sr George Blunt & my Lady if they

Lady Anne Seymour, wife of the third Baronet. Portrait by Knoyle

should be in the country tender them the choyce service of your most Affectionate
E. W. Seymour

Letter from Sir Edward to the Lady Anne Seymour, March 27th, 1662
Box 50

A folded sheet with red seal, broken, of course, and impressions impossible to decipher.

Address: For the Lady Ann Seymour
at Berry Pomeroy in Devon
ffor the Post M^r of Totness
ffranck
E. W. Seymour

My Heart

Every hour increaseth Neds undutifulness I cannot express how ungratefull he is, and that which adds to my affliction is the generall resentment of the whole towne of his high ingratitude, he hath lost himself now with those who formerly had a good esteem for him. I must wholely rely upon A supply from the Country, all other possibility fayling here. Here is no news since my last but the death of the Bishopp of Winchester ffor Gods sake haste to me, that I may speed into the Country, & fail not to send me up by the next post the Articles between S^r Wm Wal^r and myselfe ffor I am resould to seeke remedy though by an after game. My Duke is pretty weel recovered & the Queene is expected here about the 21st of Aprill. You shall here constantly from me by every Post. Dyrect your letters to be left at the Parliamt House, and not to Mr. Adams his house, wch doth retard their delivery.
Your
E. W. Seymour

Box 53
Letters from 3rd Baronet to his Wife
Address: For the Lady Anne Seymour att
Berry Pomeroy in Devon
For the Post Mr of Tottness
Franck
E. W. Seymour

London 29 Of March 1662

My Heart

It is impossible to imagine to what Height of Pride and undutifullness Ned is arrived at. He went this morning for Bradly yesterday I sent Ralph to him for the twenty pounds I lent him since I could not recover one penny of the portion. His answer was he had no money neither should I ever have A farthing from him. My Ld Sterlin(?) is now at my elbow pressing me with such(?) importunitys that I am ashamd to heare. I must be forced to deliver upp my bargaine againe and loose the money already payd. Ned hath pd my bro. Th. Trelawny 1300 lb in full and would have the indgent(?) made over to Mr. Clayton so that the charge should still remain at his dispose, many more such base actions he attempts not fitting to be named amongst christians or civill men. I must be forced to A sute both with him and his father in law, of the success I have very good hopes from the incouragement of Mr. Maynard. I expected to have heard from Giles Wolfe, but his son hath got the crampe. Pray let me hear from you suddenly and effectually. I will write this post to Wm. Carter at Bradly to whom I hope you have given directions concerning the goods there. There is nothing happened since my last worth yr knowledge I have written constantly by every post. My Lord Duke of Albemarle is very well recovered. I am
        your E. W. Seymour

I was yesterday with Mr. Adrian May his Burrowh Ducks sett a brood but all the rest of the fowle lay store of Eggs except the black necks.

Assure my neighbour Bogan I will effectually effect his desires in his letter exprest. My Ld Marquess his bill for sale of lands hath been twice read, I think ther will be scarce enough to make A house on Thursday, by which meanes the courtiers sway and rule the rost and the Bill for uniformity is as I heare finisht by the house of Peeres, and will not be sent to us on thursday next.

London 21 of June 1662

My Heart

I have been every day in expectation of some conclusion of the unfortunate differences between my selfe and most undutifull sonne but as yet I cannot give you any comfort, neither indeed can I hope from so much obstinacy any fillial complyance. But as Piggs which devoure Acornes, & never looke to the tree from whence they fell. I

last night attended Judge Windham with Sr Peter Buller this day my sonn Ned and Mr. Clayton ar to conferr with Sr Peter and on munday Judge Windeham & Sr Peter Bath ar to be attended on by S^r Wm Walr and his Councell, who I am confident would be reasonable but for Neds untowardness and instigation(?). Be the event what it will I will hasten home to wch end by (deleted) next post I will dyrect you where my horses shall meet me. I was this day seven night which was the last Saturday upon the scaffold where I saw Sr Hen. Vane's head severd from his shoulders. Yesterday ther was one of the Portugall ladys wch came over wth the Queene had A young baby dropt from her at Court. The Queene perfectly recovered. Cherryes ar cryed heer in the streets for A penny A pound. Will Carter will give A more full Account wch makes me conclude the sooner. I shall desyre the tender of my services to all my friends & that you will take care my horses be in the best condition they may for A speedy iourney
   Your owne
          E. W. Seymour

Address:
These ffor ye Honourable Sr Edward
Seymo^r at Bery Pomeroy
Leave these with ye postmaster of
Totnes to be sent with care
and speed

                                          Totnes
                               post ii pd fr. Exon
Honourable S^r

   Riding hither to Exeter, accidentally I met with y^r eldest son, and falling into some discourse about y^r grand differences, I found him to deliver himselfe with so much candour and moderation yt I could not refraine to give you (by post) an account thereof. His thoughts run altogether upon the preservation of the Honour of you^r Noble ffamily, and you^r owne particular repute and safety, and how he may prevent all false & injurious reports that may be given out agt either yo^{r}selfe or him, by persons ignorant, or not thoroughly acquainted with the whole case or controversy. to work out those ends if a necessity of reconciliation: and I am glad that having but mentioned a reformed(?) he was pleasd to hearken to me, and to yield to my desires and this he is contented to do, namely, that any man of honor or estimacn and sound judgment shall determine the question, I thought the Bishop of Exon, & I suppose that the naming(?) of that person might invite you to an acceptacion of a reference(?) yr son will acquiesce in his decision whether your dispute may not be fayrely ended by such a Reverend Prelate who cannot abide here in Exon till you answer my letter by y^r presence or yr son, whch I presume you may do by tomorrow night. Lett me beg you if possible that you would come yourselfe.

 accidit in puncto, quod non speratur in anno
        Will. Jesson

From ye Dolphin
Exon, Jan. 12th
1662

6. Sir Edward Seymour (VI) (1633-1707). 4th Baronet

The blame for the present condition of Berry Pomeroy Castle can, I feel, be laid fairly and squarely upon the shoulders of the fourth baronet. He deserted the old home of his fathers and allowed it to be demolished bit by bit, preferring to settle his wife and family at Maiden Bradley in Wiltshire. On account of this he really ought not to be placed among the generations who lived at Berry. He was probably born there, however, and so did reside there in early life. Consideration of the man and his brilliant career are also not without interest to the reader. Sir Edward was a fine politician and when his father died, and he inherited the baronetcy, he was fifty-five years of age, and at the height of his fame. It was not therefore likely that a country seat in so remote a place as Devonshire would appeal to him at all. Then again, neither of his sons wanted the castle, so whilst holding on to the estate he abandoned the castle. Prince laments that the same generation which saw it rise to its meridian saw its eclipse. A strange happening indeed, and one which succeeding generations have never ceased to regret. I expect, too, that by 1688 the buildings were in poor shape. The previous baronet had lost a fortune in the Royalist cause and was no doubt impoverished for the rest of his life. It is unlikely that he was able to maintain so large a building in good condition. So its poor state may have been another factor which swayed the 4th baronet against maintaining it.

It is easy to pass on to the more distinguished actions of Sir Edward, for he was a truly great man, and a most interesting character. He was referred to by Guthrie as "the great Sir Edward". The writer of the "Annals" comments, "Few private gentlemen in England ever had so large or so continued a share in public transactions as he had, for, from the time of the Restoration (when he was 27 years of age) to the time of his death, he was a member of the English Parliament, always representing the city of Exeter, except on three occasions when he was returned for Hindon, Devon and Totnes. It has been generally agreed that he had a great command of speech, and that his eloquence was of a style particularly adapted to the English House of Commons. In consequence he became of the highest importance to the Court upon any emergency, and, being possessed of plenty of spirit, he was always either the first man in the Ministry or the Leader of the Opposition."

In 1673 he was unanimously elected Speaker of the House of Commons. He seems to have been an arrogant and proud man and the anecdotes related of him are numerous. There is space here for a couple only. On a certain occasion when driving to the House of Commons his coach broke down, whereupon he ordered his coachman to stop the very first coach he saw. This was done and Sir Edward immediately turned out the protesting occupant saying, 'Sir, it is far better for you to walk than the Speaker of the House of Commons!" On another occasion he was talking to the Prince of Orange, who had but just arrived in England. The Prince for the sake of conversation remarked to him, "Sir, I believe you are of the same family as the Duke of Somerset", whereupon Sir Edward turned upon him saying, "Your Majesty is misinformed; the Duke of Somerset is of my family". He never forgot that his was the senior branch of the Seymours.

He refused a Barony which Queen Anne would have bestowed upon him. Was it because he thought that the Dukedom of Somerset might soon be restored to the senior branch of the Seymours? In this he would have been right because the male line of the junior branch failed in his grandson's time, and it was he, the sixth baronet, who eventually became the 8th Duke of Somerset. This was in 1750, almost two centuries after the execution of the first Duke, the Lord Protector.

CHAPTER 4
THE FOLKLORE

The subject is a fascinating one and the canvas large. Every country has its distinctive folklore with a flavour all its own. The stories have been woven into music, books and poetry. The folklore of the Rhine has been immortalised in Wagner's operas, whilst Grieg charmed the world with his many dainty settings in music of the Scandinavian sagas. Much has been written upon the subject in the present century, and the more one reads the more one becomes convinced that the stories handed on from one generation to another are necessary to all races. They come from the never-never land which existed long ago and to which it is good for men sometimes to retreat. Romance, drama, high chivalry — all are there. The happy ending for the lovers, a crown for the valiant, the triumph of good over evil — all these things existed as a matter of course in that dim and distant past of long ago.

An interesting point is the fact that mankind has a strong desire to be at one with these epic stories, and will carry them forward in time almost to the present generation. Fantastic stories are soon woven round those who have a personality strong enough to have stolen the limelight in their day. Endless anecdotes, both true and untrue, surround the indomitable character of a Sir Winston Churchill, for instance. Such people become legends in their own lifetime and soon have a permanent place in folklore.

One of the pleasing attributes of this subject is surely the fact that exaggeration plays a definite part in every one of the stories, and it is surely this very thing which lifts them high above our mundane existence. Mankind at its best craves an exalted life, and it is this which the legends attached to each race of men supplies. They are refreshing in their directness and simplicity.

The south-west is rich in folklore; some has a touch of the sublime, such as the stories of King Arthur and his knights of the Round Table, whilst others like the doings of Tom Pearce's Grey Mare are ridiculous and no more. Sometimes the stories are similar and repeat in different localities. Most places have one or two apocryphal tales to relate of the dim and distant past. Dartmoor is fortunate in possessing legends of great variety, such as those which tell of Childe the Hunter, the wish-hounds or Binjie Gear, who haunts Cranmere Pool as a black colt. I would claim, however, that the Castle of Berry Pomeroy has more fantastic tales attached to it than anywhere else in the southwest. Whilst some are but trivial yet others are folklore in the really grand manner — both dramatic and poignant. Just why such stories have attached themselves to this particular castle one cannot attempt to explain. They are there for us to consider whether we like it or not, and no book on the castle would be complete without them.

The age of the stories must vary considerably. Some may even ante-date the castle itself and come down to us from primitive times, whilst others cannot be more than a century or so in age. I shall attempt to show how even at this moment the stories are growing and gathering details which were never heard of when I was a boy. But this is one of the fascinating attributes of folklore — it grows as time goes on.

The Wishing Tree

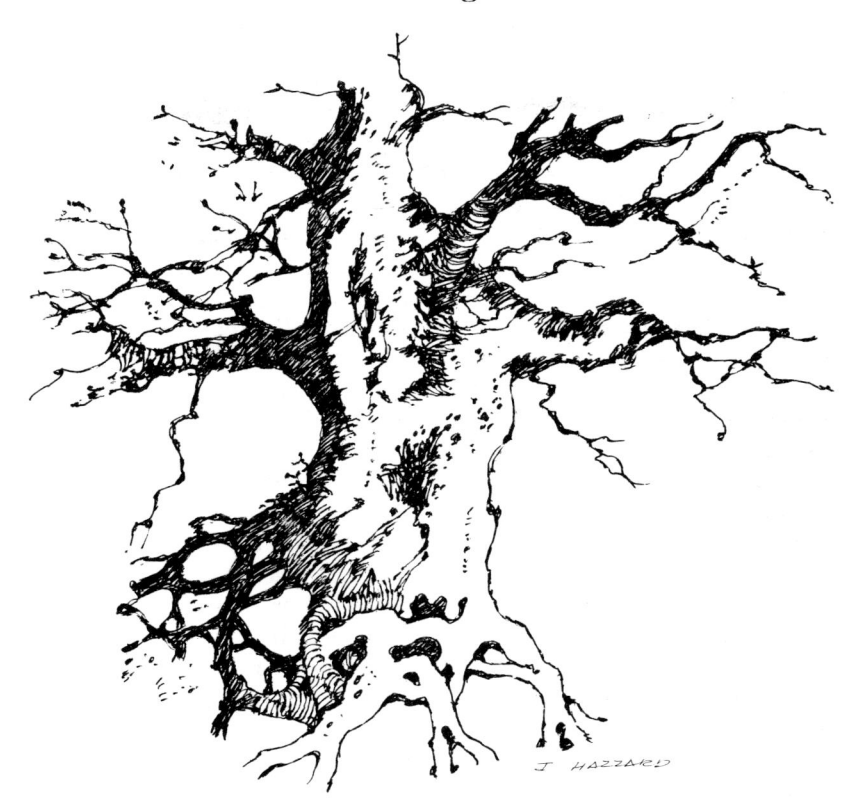

On the eastern side of St. Margaret's Tower, upon the path which descends steeply to the Gatcombe Brook, there used to stand the remains of a giant beech tree. Only the gnarled stump of this huge tree remained, and it stood on the left hand side as you went down the path, about 30 yards from the top. This was the old Wishing Tree. If you went round it three times backwards in the direction of the sun you would get your wish, providing that you kept it a secret. A nice variant mentioned in Wishart's novel "A Secret of Berry Pomeroy" was that you had to be blindfolded as well. Since the trunk stood on a precipitous slope and had a large circumference, a great deal of stamina was needed; but if you performed the feat blindfolded, then it was quite dangerous as well. The tree was marked on large scale maps and was said to be older than the castle itself. The novelist, Mrs. Bray of Tavistock, visited it in 1838 and considered it "by no means of such great antiquity". Note that in the fabulous age of the wishing tree we have a secondary strand of folklore.

By the early 1970s the huge trunk of this tree finally rotted away and today not a vestige of it is left. But did the story die? Not a bit of it! Someone feeling that the castle would not be the castle without its Wishing Tree attached a notice to a young beech at the top of the path. You will guess that it bore the legend "Wishing Tree", and I saw an earnest young woman only the other day walking backwards round its trunk. So this piece of folklore was jealously preserved for generations to come by one who felt that it must not be allowed to die out.

I have placed this story first because it may well be the oldest of the Berry Pomeroy legends. It is well known that in pre-Christian days trees, as well as standing stones, were often venerated, and to dance round them was an established custom. In later times to go round them backwards was to summon the Devil, and this legend attaches itself to Chanctonbury Ring in Sussex. So somewhere just below where the castle now is, in prehistoric times, there may have stood a stone or a tree that was venerated. It seems that it is the story which is older than the castle and not the tree.

The Invincible Castle

The actual castle of Berry Pomeroy and the castle as it appears in folklore are two very different things. The one was after all of no great strength as castles go, but the other was an impregnable fortress from which knights in armour rode forth to do battle in splendid array. Here a mighty siege took place, so that according to one source men died in their thousands. Here the haughty Pomeroys held sway for nearly five centuries — their power all but regal. Here two brothers of the house spurred their horses over the cliff on which the castle stands, braving certain death rather than surrender to the foes which beset them. Here prisoners at all times were treated with horrid cruelty. Here unnatural things happened —

Bird's Eye view of castle

a father getting his own daughter with child, a maiden starved to death in a dungeon by her jealous sister. In the earth rich treasure lies awaiting discovery, whilst secret passages beneath the castle led to other ancient houses and churches. The Pomeroys of this castle lived in splendour, riding roughshod over any who were foolish enough to resist them. As the legends approach more modern times, so a way had to be found in folklore to explain away the sorry ruin which we see today. It is disposed of in two ways — first the rather unheroic story that the castle was bombarded from the hill to the north-west by Cromwell's cannons — secondly (and surely much more gloriously) that it was destroyed by a terrible conflagration which broke out at the height of a violent thunderstorm, when the scathing lightning fired the buildings. So in folklore the invincible castle is overcome at last by the fury of the elements and perishes in a mass of flames which devour everything. In these legends nothing good or happy occurs at any time; all is sinister and macabre. Two salient facts shine through the gloom — the invincibility of the castle, and the superb strength of the Pomeroys who owned it.

These are the principle legends which have come down to us; presently they will each be considered separately, but for the moment they have been presented as a woven tapestry which enshroud the ruins at the present time. One must point out at once that the sadness of the folklore has no counterpart in the actual story of the castle, so far as can be seen. It was owned and lived in by only two families, the Pomeroys and the Seymours, and the doings of each generation of them is very well documented, with the exception of the first one or two. We see them to have been almost entirely gentry who devoted their lives to their county and country. They were sheriffs very often, and sometimes members of Parliament, and appear to have lived normal lives which in no way reflected the extravagantly gloomy legends which surround their home. Indeed the story of the historical castle and the story of the castle in folklore are quite incompatible. All one can say in conclusion is, that the men of old in this particular corner of Devon longed for a stronghold to which they could repair in times of peril, if not in fact then in fancy. So in Berry Castle they refused to see anything but a glorious fortress, mighty and unassailable.

The Great Siege

The legend of a great siege is puzzling because if it ever took place it could not have been in historical times. There is no documentary evidence of such an event. The political storms of bygone centuries passed Berry Pomeroy by. Some writers have assumed that it took place during the Western Rising of 1549, when Sir Thomas Pomeroy fought for the rebels. But he sold the manor and castle in 1548, so could not have been there to be besieged. Yet others have made this the occasion of the death-leap of the Pomeroy brothers; but once again the date makes this an absurd suggestion. Then again in the days of the Civil War the Roundheads are credited with besieging the castle. But historians of the campaign in the south-west make no mention of any such siege. The Seymours were then still engaged upon an ambitious rebuilding programme, and by that time would have demolished the old curtain wall on the south side between the gatehouse and the kitchen, to make way for new buildings which in point of fact, never took shape. I believe that at the time of the Civil War the castle was therefore indefensible. Such a staunch royalist as the second baronet would surely have defended his castle for the King if the thing had been practical. But it was not; and that is why in 1642 a party of Roundhead soldiers, in the absence of the baronet and his son, were able to walk into the castle, and help themselves to goods to the value of £89. 12s. 6d.

Now the tradition of the great siege is very strong; so what conclusions are we to draw? Can we say that there was a castle here in the dark ages, or perhaps a strong earthwork, as far back as prehistoric days? Fortunately we do not have to believe in any such things, for there is not a shred of evidence to support them.

Now it is well known in the study of folklore that events of marked similarity attach themselves to different places. There are instances of this in Devon, and it could have happened here. In the year 851 a great battle against invading Danes was fought and won at Wicganbeorg. The site of this battle has been debated, but Professor W.G. Hoskins (p.52 'Devon') favours Weekaborough — a spot only a mile or so north of the castle. Here are today the farms of Higher and Lower Weekaborough, which, with cottages now gone, once made up a village. Some research on the writer's part brought to light two adjacent fields close by, both of which were called

Battlebury. Then again on the other side of the Totnes-Newton Abbot main road was the farm of Battleford. Its farmhouse, destroyed by fire some years ago, has now vanished, but the name remains on old maps. The battle was fought most probably over quite a wide area. At Weekaborough one looks in vain for an old earthwork to provide the 'burgh' or stronghold with a stout bank, but none is to be seen. Beside Higher Weekaborough, however, there is a steep conical hill which could have been a defensible place for the Saxons to hold, and this could have been besieged. I offer the suggestion that in folklore the real site of the battle has been transferred to the castle over the years; for no sooner was it built than it would become in mens' minds the strong place, the fortress of the neighbourhood, and so the undefended hill at Weekaborough could in time have been forgotten.

The Pomeroys in Folklore

The Pomeroy family held the castle for 19 generations, from soon after the Norman Conquest to the year 1548; so it is only to be expected that they have a very definite niche in the legends which surround their former home. Not so the Seymours who succeeded them, for not a single heroic tale attaches itself to them. I have drawn attention elsewhere to the fact that when they purchased Berry Pomeroy they would be regarded at first with suspicion, for the family had hitherto had no connection with Devonshire. So in the mid 16th century the former landlords would be looked back upon with affection, and it would not be long before in the eyes of the peasantry, they became legends; tales about them would be discussed, exaggerated and pass into folklore. The Pomeroys thus became fabulous, so that when in the 19th century people began to write about the castle, they were told tales of the mighty barons who at one time dwelt there in almost regal splendour, and how their stronghold on its lofty crag had proved quite invincible. The visitors who began to drive over at the beginning of the century from the new resort of Torquay were only too ready to believe in these men of might and substance; so delighted were they with the romantic ruin that they were prepared to think that almost anything could have happened there.

The Pomeroys have been fortunate in having so excellent a historian as Edward B. Powley, who in his 'The House of de la Pomerai' has recorded the doings of each generation after what must have been much painstaking research. He traces the family from the Norman Conquest to modern times, and even on to the other side of the Atlantic where Pomeroys still flourish. He shows us, in contrast to the folklore about them, a race of dignified country gentry who concerned themselves for the most part with the affairs of the county. Some were knights, a few were members of Parliament, and some Sheriffs of the county. None were raised to the peerage, and only two achieved notoriety — the second Sir Henry and the last Sir Thomas. The first has been fully discussed already and the second, who backed the wrong side in the Western Rebellion of 1549, was lucky to have escaped the horrid fate of being hanged, drawn and quartered as his associates were. The Pomeroys made no great alliances, but married into the local families of the south-west. Such men as these were the very backbone of the country — loyal and dependable.

Yet in folklore, as you will see, the most fantastic tales attached themselves to the family. Even today the legends tend to grow. Only the other day a friend of mine began to speak of a branch of the family who were once neighbours of his. "Great big chaps they were" he said; "One was a pilot in the last war and he did the most amazing things". "Stop!" I cried, "You are making them into legendary people". And so he was. The folklore about the Pomeroys was taking shape right before my eyes!

Pomeroy's Leap

Just where the escarpment on which the castle stands is steepest is the spot, below the northern corner, named on large scale maps "Pomeroy's Leap". Here in folklore was enacted the most dramatic of the legends attached to Berry Pomeroy; for the story goes that two brothers, the last of their line, rather than surrender to the foes which beset them, arrayed themselves in full armour, and having blindfolded their chargers, spurred them on over the precipice — thus riding to certain death. After the fearful act had been committed the enemy permitted their retainers to go from the castle

Pomeroys Leap

to recover the bodies in peace, after which they were given honourable burial in the castle.

Mrs. Combes of Totnes, the 19th century poetess wrote: —

"What vision this mine eyes assail?
I see a mother, hear her wail,
Her noble boys, her all,
Hem'd in by rebels conquering bands
Rather than in their foemen's hands
Alive they prisoners fall,
Down o'er the cliff they ride to die,
There side by side their corses lie,
Fame shall their praises sing."

A weaker version of the same story has only one rider, and that was Sir Henry (2) de la Pomerai. After the return of King Richard I from captivity Sir Henry, who had rebelled against him during his absence, returned in haste to his castle from Cornwall where he had been at St. Michael's Mount. Here after a few days appeared the King's Herald. Sir Henry entertained him, but the Herald soon declared his real mission, which was to arrest Sir Henry. The latter is then said to have stabbed the Herald in rage, killing him on the spot. Then, realising that all was lost, he mounted his charger, forcing him to leap over the edge of the cliff. Mrs. Bray, the novelist in her book "Sir Henry de Pomeroy" makes use of this story, and one must give her full marks for the splendid way in which she handles it, bringing her novel to a thrilling conclusion. Arthur Mee in his "Devon" adds a nice touch to the story, for he says that Sir Henry, just before the death leap "sounded a blast on his horn". I wonder where he got this final touch of melodrama, for it lifts the story to the heights of a Wagnerian opera.

It is quite disappointing to have to state that neither version of the story could be true. The end of Sir Henry was certainly not so glorious as this. It seems he had turned out the monks at St. Michael's Mount which he fortified. On hearing that the King was about to return, according to Houdene (iii 238), he died of fright. Another version of the story is that he severed a vein and so died from loss of blood. But the main thing against the death-leap story is that the event would have ante-dated the building of the castle by at least a century, Henry dying c.1194, which was the year in which his son succeeded to his lands.

As to the legend of the two brothers, there is no record of any of the Pomeroys meeting a violent death; neither is there evidence, according to the pedigree of the family, as given by Powley, of two brothers being the last of the line. How then did these stories of horsemen leaping over the precipice arise? To return once more to the Battle of Wicganbeorg, which was fought over adjacent country, it might be reasonable to suppose that two horsemen, being chased by the enemy, did ride over the precipice in a desperate attempt to escape. Succeeding generations would soon make them into Pomeroys! This is no more than a suggestion, of course, but it does seem as though two riders must at some time have plunged over the edge to give rise to the legend which has fascinated succeeding generations for so long.

It must be mentioned in passing that the poem 'The Rhyme of the Duchess May' by Elizabeth Barrett Browning bears more than a passing resemblance to the story of Pomeroy's Leap. It tells the story of the castle of Linteged which is besieged. Sir Guy, the owner, knowing that he can sustain the siege no longer decides to leap on horseback from the highest tower of the castle into the ravine below. The object was to save the lives of his men, who would then be spared from the vengeance of the besieging army. His wife, the Duchess May, entices the horse up various spiral staircases to the top of the tower. Here Sir Guy mounts and with great difficulty gets the animal to spring over into space. At the last moment the Duchess jumps up behind him, and together they leap to their doom.

Now the poetess lived at Torquay from 1838-41 and it is quite likely that she visited Berry Pomeroy and heard the legend. The story, she says, was told to her in a churchyard whilst a bell was tolling — indeed a refrain "Toll slowly" occurs after every half verse of the poem, enhancing the melancholy story. Why she called the castle Linteged is at the moment an intriguing mystery, for there does not seem to be any such place. The poem appeared in 1844, and although I have consulted the London Browning Society no light has been shed on the origin of this poem. Is it yet another case of the repetition of folklore in quite different localities, or did Elizabeth Barrett Browning elaborate upon the story of Pomeroy's Leap?

The Imprisonment of Lady Margaret

This is one of the best known stories of the castle. In the Middle Ages two sisters of the household fell in love with the same man. Lady Eleanor, the elder, and owner of the castle, removed her sister, Lady Margaret, by imprisoning her in a dungeon in the tower which bears her name to this day. Now folklore, unlike the proverbial rolling stone, gathers much moss over the years; and this story is no exception. By the time of the Rev. J. Prince (he wrote in 1701) the tower had become St. Margaret's Tower, so the poor lady had become beatified. About 20 years ago I heard for the first time that she had been starved to death. Then in 1979, to crown all, I learnt that she had been walled up. What will happen to her next I can hardly wait to hear! The story is thus a good example of how folklore can expand and grow over the years, even in modern times.

You will look in the Pomeroy pedigree in vain, however, for a Lady Eleanor and a Lady Margaret who were sisters. Only once did a daughter inherit, and her name was Joanna. We are once more up against a reason for such a story. In this case we simply do not know of one.

An elaborated version of this legend is told in 'The Castle of Berry Pomeroy' by Edward Montague which is discussed elsewhere. In this variation of the story the Lady Margaret is kept by the Abbot of Torre (there called Ford Abbey) with the connivance of Lady Eleanor, in a vault near the castle chapel, which is beneath the main building. This version has a happy ending for Lady Margaret, for she is discovered by her lover. The unnatural sister and the Abbot are brought to trial. She was packed off to a nunnery, but he was buried alive.

The Unfortunate Lovers

A feud is said to have raged for years between the Pomeroys and another local family — we do not know which. It happened that a certain fair daughter of the house fell deeply in love with a youth of the rival family. The lovers used to meet clandestinely in the castle grounds. These secret meetings were discovered by the lady's brother, who one day surprised them together, and stabbed them both to death.

This is yet another gloomy legend for the truth of which no one can vouch. It is nevertheless much more likely to be founded on fact than some of the fantastic stories of Berry Pomeroy.

The Silver Spurs

In her novel 'Sir Henry de Pomeroy' the authoress, Mrs. Bray, writes as follows on p.103:- "and Sir Henry's silver spurs were won in fight by our renowned ancestor, Ralph de Pomeroy, at the Battle of Tours from an infidel leader whom he slew. He laid them at the feet of his commander, Charles Martel. Charles Martel himself buckled them on Sir Ralph, who vowed that ever after the silver spurs should be the pledge of honour with all descendants of his house, and that if anyone bearing the name of Pomeroy should be accused of a breach of good faith, he should instantly give in token one of these silver spurs, and either retrieve it with his honour, or forfeit his life in the attempt." And on p.287:- "Sir Henry would gaze long upon the portrait of a stern warrior of his race bearing in his hands a hawk and the silver spurs, whose spirit was said to wander through the castle halls to give intimation of the approaching fate of one of his descendants". Lastly on p.292:- "He saw and felt a cold shudder creep through every vein, as he recognised in the red mantle, the hawk on the wrist, and the silver spurs depending from the chain held in the right hand, the death-like and fixed countenance, the figure of that de Pomeroy represented in the picture, and to whose visitations to this world so fearful a portent was annexed".

This is an intriguing story and one would give much to know

whether it was the product of Mrs. Bray's fertile imagination. I have so far not come across the story elsewhere, but that does not mean to say that Mrs. Bray was not told it on her visit to Berry Pomeroy, and so wove it into her novel, placing it just before Sir Henry's mad death-leap.

The Kidnapped Heiress

This story is the subject of a poem by Luke M. Combes which is discussed in another chapter. It tells of the times of King Richard I's capture by the Duke of Austria whilst on a Crusade. With him was Sir Anselm de Pomeroy who was absent from his castle for so long that he was presumed dead. His daughter, Lady Margaret, thus became the heiress of all her father's estates. A conspiracy was entered into by the Prior of Modbury and the Abbots of Buckfast and Torre. They planned to kidnap her and place her in a nunnery; her lands would then become the property of the Church. She is therefore abducted, although her faithful hound, Damon, tries to protect her. He is nevertheless overcome, and she is taken to a cell by means of an underground passage which leads from the castle to Torre Abbey. Her lover spends much time in finding her. Meanwhile Sir Anselm returns and together they traverse the passage until they find her cell. Eventually she marries her lover; so in folklore the story has a happy ending. The story bears a likeness to the one previously related about the imprisoned Lady Margaret in that the name of the heroine is the same, and she also was imprisoned. There the similarity ends, however, and it seems that in folklore the name of Margaret is always attached to an imprisoned maiden — at any rate at Berry Pomeroy.

The story is most unlikely because a study of the family shows no owner of the castle by the name of Anselm, and no heiress of the name of Margaret. Torre Abbey was not in existence at the time of that Crusade, neither was the castle, if we accept post 1300 as the date of its building. This may once again be a case of a legend transferred from one place to another.

The Unwanted Child

This tale of great misery concerns an unfortunate daughter of the house. She is said to have borne an unwanted child which was sired by her own father. In her despondency she is said to have smothered it in one of the bedchambers of the castle. Nothing is known of the date of this event, neither are the names of those concerned preserved in the story. Its survival is interesting because it demonstrates that the misdoings of the Pomeroys were not glossed over in folklore, but were handed on beside the more heroic deeds of the family.

Hidden Treasure

In this story we have an example of folk memory which relates how, before the Pomeroy brothers leapt over the precipice, they buried their treasure within the castle precincts. As Mrs. Cumings's poem has it they

"First buried in the soil
What foes had fought for — gold and spoil".

One version of the story relates how there was a crock of gold hidden in the kitchen chimney. Behind the kitchen fireplace within the house there is a small, invisible chamber behind the fireplace. It was lit by a very small window which is still in situ. It is, however, secret no longer, for the wall has either fallen away or been taken down, thus revealing this 'secret' chamber.

Mrs. Cumings's poem which shows us how this attractive piece of folklore was related over a century ago has a humour all its own and is worth recording:—

"This rumour, then so widely known
Into the neighb'ring towns had flown,
And peasants, and the idle poor,
All loathing work, and loving gain,
Would oft discuss the ancient lore,

And wonder if there could be found
Without much labour, loss or pain
A treasure hidden underground;
And one who better days had known,
Went there to lodge by night and day;
Went there to dig, and weird and lone
He frightened all who passed that way.
But years before this wight was born
A peasant rose at earliest dawn
For thrice within the night he dreamed
That he must with the dawn of day
To Pomeroy Castle make his way;
A call from heaven it seemed,
At least so much impelled, that he
Firmly believed that he should be
Rewarded, and should realise
His brightest hopes, and gain a prize.
   *   *   *   *   *
Resolved, he took the nearest track,
With fitting tools upon his back,
And as he trudged his way along
He met a burly country squire —
Thus putting out his humdrum song—
Who stopped him and must needs enquire
'Where he was going that early morn,
'Ere dews were dry, or sun was born,
'Art going to work upon this track
'With pick and shovel on thy back?
'I thought that thou hadst laid them by
'And parish rates thy wants supply.'
Such men as these were then put down
By lofty menace, scoff or frown;
With these combined he did compel
The quarryman his dream to tell:
Told him the place would surely fall,
That all the treasure he would gain
Was ridicule, and loss, and pain;
Threatened to cudgel him withal:
In short such rhetoric employed
As finally his dupe decoyed

To turn at once and go to bed,
Now—who was he, who went—instead.
When the last fading rays of light
His mother had not known the one,
In his disguise, for her own son;
And over all a cloak he wore,
Concealing miner's spade and bore;
His nerves were firm, his pulse was strong
And thus equipped he stole along,
With stealthy steps made good his way,
Through Berry where the ruins lay.
Gossips relate, when centuries meet,
The shades of the departed greet
Each other in the midnight air,
And that such trysting place was there.

No such puerile fancies then,
Disturbed this man, nor fear of men,
But little knew that one was there
Concealed within a dungeon near,
Who hearing footsteps coming on,
Though in a paralysis of fear,
Had longing, dying, wish to see
Who he who thus forestalled should be,
Had cautiously—how cautiously! drawn near.
A sudden flash from lanthorn fire
Showed the suspected one, the squire.

If Argus had one hundred eyes,
Rumour a thousand tongues supplies;
But whether either of the twain
Obtained the prize they hoped to gain,
As in his dream one saw it hid,
In an old crock without a lid,
The doubtful chronicler of old,
Deposes not, nor could have told.

The squire, the peasant, both are laid
Within the nearest churchyard soil,
Where death hath no distinction made
In the rich man, or him of toil."

Folklore and wishful thinking go hand in hand, and the legend of hidden gold somewhere in the old castle always intrigues the newcomer. As I gaze upon those broken walls I often wonder how much the hope of a remote chance of discovering something fired the enthusiasm of those who, from the eighteenth century onward, used this place as a stone quarry.

Secret Passages

In folklore secret passages radiate underground from the castle to various old houses, churches and monasteries—in particular Torre Abbey. These passages are said to have been a labyrinth in which it was easy to get lost. Writers with fertile imagination have introduced large halls and cells opening out from the passages.

Just like the story of hidden treasure, this legend is quite unremarkable, for it occurs frequently where old buildings are concerned. In this particular case it is just one more instance of the certainty of exciting things existing and happening in connection with this particular castle. Of course the Pomeroys must have had secret passages by which they could travel clandestinely to just whatever destination their intrigues demanded! The novels and poems discussed in this book make much of the existence of a chapel, tombs, vaults and passages beneath the castle.

Such stories may be founded on fact in this way—old buildings of any size often had quite elaborate and ingeniously constructed sewers beneath them, and so in many cases passages really do exist, but they were utilitarian and usually fairly short in extent. The solid rock on which the castle stands, still visible as outcrops in several places, does not predispose one to believe in vaults; yet a drainage system there must have been, and one day it will probably be discovered. Caverns beneath the buildings are also not to be ruled out in a district which abounds in such things.

The Bombardment by the Roundheads

From the Middle Ages and the Pomeroys the folklore now wends its way to the 17th century. The days of high chivalry are past; knights in armour ride out from Berry no more. Bows and arrows are no longer to be found in the castle armoury, for their place has been taken by gunpowder, muskets and cannon balls. You would think that nothing more could be added to the legends of the castle. That surely all belongs to the glamorous past. But you will be wrong, for in every generation the folklore of Berry Pomeroy has to remain true to type. We see before us a gaunt ruin, and so the great question to be answered is what happened to the castle. In folklore it is disposed of in two ways—firstly by bombardment, and secondly by fire; both are dramatic enough, you must admit.

Let us consider the first story. When Mrs. Bray visited the castle in 1838 she was told by the guide that Roundhead troops, in the Civil War, placed their cannon on the hill beyond the Gatcombe Brook and destroyed the new wing recently built by Sir Edward Seymour. Notice that she was not told of a fire. Destruction by bombardment seems at first sight to be a most plausible explanation. There stand the melancholy stacks of masonry which alone survive to tell the tale. But somehow it isn't good enough on account of the cross walls which we should expect to find standing. But only a fragment of one is there. They would not stand the full force of the cannonade because it would have hit them end on; so they should still be there; but they are not. Then again there were huge windows in this wing, so that the frontage facing the fury of the enemy would present more window than wall. But the mullions would have been very massive; yet there is not a fragment of a window remaining. If this story is true the cannons did a very tidy job—too tidy, one feels. Above all, in the written history of the campaign in the south-west not a word is said of an attack on Berry Pomeroy Castle; yet the besieging of smaller houses such as Canonteign is recorded. Even the neighbouring farmhouse of Dornafield in Ipplepen is known to have been the scene of a skirmish, and three cannonballs used to be preserved in the porch there as proof.

Earlier in this chapter I have advanced the theory that I do not believe Berry Pomeroy Castle could offer any resistance at that time—the reason being that the curtain wall of the Pomeroy period, which it is reasonable to think surrounded the old castle, had been demolished to make way for new buildings. Those between the kitchen and the gatehouse were never to be completed. Then again, the third baronet lived on here until his death in 1688; he surely did not live in a ruin for over thirty years. There is also an Inventory of 1688 which records the rooms in the castle and their contents. Counting servants quarters there are over 40 of them, and there is certainly nothing like that in the remaining house. Clearly this Inventory is not of a partial ruin. I will credit the story of the bombardment when the first cannon ball is found!

The story of the bombardment cannot have gained credence until at least a couple of generations after the Civil War, and so could be of early 18th century growth.

The Great Fire

The second way in which folklore disposes of the castle is by fire. The destruction was so complete that one might have hoped that all the macabre stories which have attached themselves to Berry Pomeroy might have perished once and for all. Wishaw in his novel "A Secret of Berry Pomeroy" describes the fire thus:— "Since its destruction by fire many years before the time I write of, Berry Pomeroy had been neglected by its owners, the Seymours, though a few rooms on the right of the great entrance were still habitable. My father well recollected the terrible thunderstorm which was the cause of the fire. He spoke of it even to this day with bated breath, as of the most fearsome sight that two generations had witnessed". A friend tells me of the existence of an old print of the castle in flames, but I have never seen it.

The sight of the elegant buildings going up in a mass of flames would certainly have been a terrible sight, and viewed from below would have been awe-inspiring. From the point of view of folklore, for the castle to perish so dramatically was exactly right, for it would appear as a sacrifice to an avenging deity. Once again it is all in the grand manner of Wagner. And folklore I believe it to be. The story of the great fire was nevertheless firmly believed in until the Department of the Environment took over the guardianship of the castle in 1977. They have carried out extensive repairs to the whole structure, and the interesting thing about their work, which at the time of writing has been going on for some four years, is this—no evidence of fire has been found so far. There is no blackening of the walls anywhere, no charred fragments of wood where the joists have been—rather pieces of wood in good condition still survive in some places. Upon the sills there is not a trace of molten lead from the windowframes. Of course, until the floors are uncovered we cannot be absolutely sure that a fire did not take place, for they will be coated with ash if it did. But at the present time it looks as though destruction by fire is the greatest of the Berry Pomeroy myths. There may have been a small fire in one of the wings which gave rise to the story, but even that looks extremely doubtful.

Bearing in mind the fact that a story of destruction by fire was not told to Mrs. Bray on her visit of 1838, or she would have been sure to have made much of it, we come back to the question that every visitor to the castle asks—what happened to it?

There is only one writer who tells us what happened and that was good old Prince, the vicar of Berry Pomeroy, for in 1701 in his "Worthies of Devon" p.492, he says quite clearly " 'tis all demolished". Yes, I believe that it was as simple as that—the castle was demolished. It had become a white elephant in the family, and so must have been something of a liability to Sir Edward Seymour, the fourth baronet, who was Speaker of the House of Commons. As a politician he had no time for country life in Devonshire and made his Wiltshire estate at Maiden Bradley his only country home. So he resolved to dismantle the old family castle, and began by demolishing the grand north-west wing which had only recently been built. The reason no doubt was that all the best things were in it. The splendid alabaster mantlepieces and the carved woodwork which Prince describes would go to other houses and fetch good money. The great windows with their coloured glass would be entirely removed, and the rest has been a most satisfactory stone quarry over the centuries. Prince in his lament for the splendid home which was no more could not very well condemn the action of Sir Edward for fear of offending the patron of his living and the landlord of his whole parish! So he evades the issue and tells us what he remembered of the magnificence of the place. Had there been a fire, rest assured he would have told us about it in his most graphic style. Note that folklore is quite silent on the real fate of the castle, for demolition was far too ignominious an end for the invincible castle.

If you have troubled to read so far you must admit that the legends which surround the castle are dramatic, powerful and very much alive. The number and variety of the stories place them amongst the best there are in the south-west. We should simply accept them and not try too hard to account for them all. As a reflection of the inventiveness of the minds of the folk hereabouts they are surely in a class of their own. They show a willingness to believe almost anything, however fantastic, about this almost palatial home which the old castle finally became. Yet in the end can we dismiss the folklore in so cavalier a fashion? The castle is a place of memories, and you will read in the next chapter of the supernatural; for this is said to be one of the most consistently haunted places in Britain—and over a long period of time, too. Here both legend and haunting go hand in hand. Does the very existence of the hauntings in a way prove the folklore to be founded on fact? Contrariwise, does the folklore, so far as it is true, pre-suppose that we shall believe more readily in the hauntings? There is much food for thought here.

Below ground-floor level: 14th century doorway in N.W. corner

CHAPTER 5

The Hauntings

Sceptics will no doubt quarrel with me for including a chapter on such a subject in a book of this kind. But it is meant to be a book which considers every aspect of the story of the castle, and the persistence of the stories of the hauntings is as much a part of the place as the folklore or the very stones of which it is composed. Mention Berry Pomeroy to any of your friends, and as likely as not you will be discussing ghosts within the next moment or two, whether you like it or not. The late Elliott O'Donnell, who wrote so much about psychic matters, related to an acquaintance of mine that he could trace the hauntings at Berry back over several centuries. Unfortunately, he never wrote about his findings, and his source of information is not known. But for such a man to have made this statement at all

White Lady

proves that the beginnings of the stories of the hauntings are, like the folklore, buried in antiquity. Also, like the folklore, they concern the Pomeroy family and not the Seymours.

The earliest ghost story which I can trace is the well known one of the visit of Dr. Farquhar to tend a sick woman at the castle, probably in the 1790's. The story is perhaps the best known of all, and will be dealt with presently. It has the ring of authenticity and, was written down in his Memoirs by this eminent physician. So this takes us back about two centuries. There are quite a few other stories from responsible witnesses, and they take us roughly up to the time of the Great War. The stories which approach our times, however, do not seem to have the same authority as the earlier ones and border on the sensational. One writer has copied another over the years, and the same stories have been repeated ad nauseam. Mediums have visited Berry from time to time and poured forth exaggerated stories of their experiences to the press. The AA's excellent "Book of British Villages" (1980) for instance states "A thousand years of history lie behind its (the castle's) grim and forbidding gatehouse, the entrance to a site often described as one of the most haunted in Britain"; and speaking of the Pomeroys and Seymours "... their ghosts are said to prowl the walls, staircases and dungeons of the castle..." Much in a similar vein has been written over the years, and it seemed to me that perhaps it amounted to very little. Were the hauntings fading? Was the remembrance of them all that was left?

Then I began to delve deeper, and to get away from what had been written. I visited people who lived close at hand, and had done for long years. Immediately I began to get results, for many such could give me first-hand information of what had happened to themselves or their friends. It was really quite astonishing, for I found that not only the old castle but also the surrounding countryside has its share of psychic phenomena—particularly the Gatcombe valley just below the ruins. As a result of this investigation one is forced to conclude that there has been no lapse in paranormal occurences at Berry after all.

The stories which I myself have investigated I now relate and will deal with the older ones towards the end of the chapter. (1) On July 18th, 1981, Mr. J. Hazzard and I visited the Castle Mill which is situated in the Gatcombe valley just below the castle. This is an ancient building in part, and is mentioned in a lease of 1467. Mr. A. Ellis, who lives at the mill and farms the adjacent land, told me how one spring evening not long ago he was ploughing the field above the mill just south of the castle. Every time he came up to the top of the hill, close to the ruins, he was beset by an icy chill and was filled with a sense of fear. This happened each time his tractor reached the highest part of the field. He finally could not stand it any longer and went home.

(2) Mr. Ellis was milking one evening at dusk in an outbuilding of the mill. He saw what he thought to be his nephew repeatedly dodging in and out of the cows and disturbing them. Finally he shouted

at him to stop it, but the figure disappeared. On entering the house he found that his nephew had never been outside at all. The figure was hooded, but resembled his nephew in build and height.

(3) Mrs. Ellis related to me how a few years ago a clergyman and his wife and daughter, who was aged about eighteen, visited the castle. They entered by the gatehouse, whereupon the daughter suddenly cried out and fainted. She was assisted to the nearby tea-room where Mrs. Ellis happened to be. The girl was brought round and said she had seen the sudden apparition of a young woman dressed in blue who had beckoned to her from the gateway. She was so frightened by this that she had fainted. Now the ghost of the woman in blue is one of the old stories of the castle, and will be mentioned later. Mrs. Ellis suggested to the girl that it was all her imagination, and that she had been reading about the castle and its ghosts. But the father assured her that until about a quarter of an hour before they had never heard of the castle of Berry Pomeroy. They had noticed a signpost and thought, just on the spur of the moment, that they would go there.

(4) Some animals are much disturbed by the castle atmosphere. Mr. Ellis's alsatian bitch, for instance, can never be persuaded to go up to the castle although she likes a walk as much as any dog. Another acquaintance of mine related how his dog, who had walked all round the ruins, was suddenly terrified when he approached the St. Margaret's Tower. Nothing would persuade him to go on, even though his master tried carrying him there.

(5) Another story was told by Mrs. Rowden, who with her husband, lived at the Castle Lodge for many years. She said that in September each year a couple, now elderly, always visit the castle. They first went there on their honeymoon at that time of the year. When going along the rampart walk towards St. Margaret's Tower their dog suddenly went mad with fear and dashed off. They themselves were surrounded by an icy blast and sense of chill. Though frightened, they stood their ground, hoping they might see something; but nothing appeared. Each year of their lives they have revisited the spot in September, but have never felt or seen anything again.

(6) Mrs. Rowden also related that in the valley below the mill there was a wooden footbridge over the brook. Here many people have seen an old lady in quaint, old fashioned garments. She is always in the centre of the bridge and is not at all alarming.

(7) The jamming of cameras and spoilt films are a regular phenomenon at Berry Pomeroy. My wife had a film of photos taken there come out as a complete blank for no reason at all. She is one of many to have suffered in this way. Others are said to have found on their photos figures which they certainly did not see at the time. I cannot give a definite example of this phenomenon, however.

(8) Not long ago a friend related to me how she first visited the castle at dusk on a summer's evening. She and her husband had entered the woods from the valley below, and as they began to climb the narrow path which leads to the castle, she was beset by a sudden feeling of great fear and oppression. She steeled herself to go on to the castle, but she did not dare to enter it. Her one desire was to get away as quickly as possible. They hurried back by the way they had come, and not until she was clear of the woods did she feel herself again.

(9) My wife remembers visiting Berry Pomeroy as a child in the company of her mother and another little friend. There was some difficulty in getting the key, and when they arrived in front of the castle Mrs. Charlesworth saw an old man cutting the grass with a scythe. He was dressed in old-fashioned garments and had a patch over one eye, which gave him a rather sinister appearance. "Run along and ask that old man if he has the key" she said. The children ran off in the direction in which she had pointed, but they could see no old man. They soon returned saying he was not there. "Don't be silly", said Mrs. Charlesworth, and went towards him. But she came slowly back to them after a moment, quite perturbed, and said, "I did not speak to him after all—he was such an evil-looking man." She certainly saw him but the children did not.

(10) The following story of the castle mill was related by Miss E. Beveridge, M.A., who once lived not far from the castle at Combe Fishacre. She writes "A South African friend was staying with me, and going out for a late afternoon run in her car, out of mere curiosity we turned down a lane I had never previously explored, leading to the castle mill of which I knew nothing. Half a mile or so along this lane my friend's easy flow of chatter died away and an uncomfortable silence ensued which I found it impossible to break. On comparing notes afterwards it seemed that we had both simultaneously become aware of something strange and oddly disquieting in the atmosphere; then I was struck by something unusual in our immediate surroundings which I could not at first identify. I

puzzled over it for a moment before I realised that the fowls scratching in a sloping field beside the track were of a breed I had never before encountered, scraggy, long-legged creatures, and in lieu of ordinary chicken houses were rough shelters of turves and branches, while certain domes of plaited straw like old-fashioned bee-skeps apparently housed a few broody hens sitting on their eggs.

It was a perfect afternoon in May, no breath of air stirred, sunlight lay warm and golden over everything; conditions could hardly have been *less* sinister, and yet there was something very eerie in the atmosphere. The silence was profound, uncannily so, for the environs of a mill even so remote and small as this.

Suddenly we rounded a corner and found ourselves in a tiny farmyard, the house to one side, some ramshackle sheds on the other and before us a swiftly flowing stream. All this I took in at a glance but in my nervous confusion I may have been mistaken in details. Was it a millstream, or merely a dark pool or pond lying dark and sinister at the foot of beetling crags?

The mill house was small, low, and indescribably shabby, with small, deepset windows overhung with ragged thatch. The only living creature, apart from some ducks dabbling in the edge of the water, was a little girl of eleven or twelve who was sitting on the low wall which partly enclosed the yard next the pool or stream. I never saw such a little savage—dirty and unkempt, with swarthy skin and coarse black hair which looked as if it had never known brush or comb, and smouldering black eyes which were fixed on us in an unwinking stare of such intense malignity that we felt ourselves more than ever intruders where we had no right to be. Her dress looked like nothing on earth but a filthy sack with holes cut in it for head and arms, and a piece of rope loosely tied about the waist. She was sitting hunched with chin on hands and elbows on knees, bare legs drawn up so that the soles of her feet were pressed vertically against the wall. Without moving a muscle she crouched there, glaring at us in a deadly silence that could be felt.

Normally we should have called a greeting and asked the name of the place, but neither of us had the nerve to break that uncanny silence, seething as it was with almost murderous hostility. "I don't like this!" Hilda muttered, starting to reverse the car in a nervous haste quite unlike her usual placidity. "Let's get out of it as quick as we can!" Somehow she managed to turn the car in the tiny yard and we shot off down the way we had come, followed to the last by that glare of hatred which would have struck us dead if looks could kill! Neither of us spoke a word until we had passed the point in the lane at which we had first fallen silent, then each drew a deep breath of relief.

"Thank Heaven we've got out of *that*!" Hilda exclaimed. "Do you know, I had a horrible feeling that we'd strayed into something, some place or time, right out of this day and age. That awful child! . . . Do you think that place is really there, or was I imagining it?"

"It's there all right," I said, "but were *we* there—then, now, or ever?"

"I see what you mean. I'm not a bit psychic or even imaginative, as you know, but that was a very queer experience and I should hate to repeat it. I was never more scared in my life! That *horrible* child—she gave me the creeps! Do you think she was a ghost? She evidently saw *us*, and hated us like poison."

"Yes, I'm sure she saw us, but I felt as though it was *we* that were the ghosts. We were on a different plane of existence, anyhow."

We both felt shaken and sobered for hours after that experience. But I had an irresistible urge to go back and have another look. I could not ask Hilda to repeat the experiment, but a fortnight later I had another visitor and decided to try what effect the place might have on her, without telling her anything about my previous visit. So, when we were out for an evening stroll, I turned without remark down the lane that led to what I shall always think of as the Haunted Mill.

At precisely the spot where on the former occasion Hilda and I had become aware of something strange in the atmosphere, Katie suddenly halted and announced that she was not going any farther. "No," in response to my query, "I'm not tired, I just don't feel like going on. There's a mill or something along there, isn't there? You go on if you like; I'll wait for you here," and she sat down on the flowery bank beside the track.

"I'd like to have a look at it," I said, "if you don't mind waiting," and I walked briskly on.

Once more it was a perfect evening, warm and still, but there was a subtle change. The air was full of the normal sounds incidental to a farm. Cows were lowing, dogs barking; a man was whistling as he crossed a field, carrying a couple of buckets, a sheepdog trotting at his heels. The strange fowls and their rude shelters had vanished, and in their place were wooden henhouses of the usual type, while

White Leghorns, Buff Orpingtons and Rhode Island Reds lined up at the hoppers for their ration of corn.

When the mill house came in sight I noticed at once that it had been completely rethatched. The roof appeared much higher, too, to provide a second storey where there could have been nothing but a loft before. The windows seemed larger, the leaded panes twinkling in the evening light where before had been dark gaping holes which I now realised had been innocent of glass. A new wing had been added, and a porch overgrown with honeysuckle or some other creeper had sprouted before the door—and all in a couple of weeks!

There was no dark, malevolent little damsel crouching on the wall, and the atmosphere was perfectly normal and serene . . .

When I got back to where my cousin was sitting she instantly scrambled to her feet with an expression of relief.

"So you *have* come back!" she exclaimed. "Do you know, I had a horrid feeling that I might never see you again! There's something queer about this place, isn't there? I hadn't the courage to go on with you, and that's the truth."

I had to admit that there *was* something very queer about it, though I could not bring myself to tell her the full story of our former adventure.

I never discovered the history of the place, but like so many of the Devon mills it may well have been there, in essentials at least, from long before the Norman Conquest. I should surmise that our swarthy little maiden was neither Norman nor Saxon, but of the dark indigenous or at least ancient British stock. There must have been many such surviving in remote places in the far west well into the 11th or 12th century, which was probably the date of our intrusion. Was that sullen child a slave in a Saxon or Norman household, whose sufferings and undying hate yet lived on to haunt unwary visitors like ourselves?"

(11) Mr. Chips Barber of Pinhoe, Exeter, related to me the other day how in April, 1963, when a boy of 13, he visited the castle with other boys. It was about six o'clock in the evening, and they were playing football on the lawn before the gatehouse. As luck would have it the ball sailed right over the wall and into St. Margaret's tower. Chips ran to retrieve it, passing the custodian who was preparing to lock the castle for the night. He could not see the ball and guessed that it had rolled down the steps to the very bottom of the tower. He scrambled down the broken stairway and, sure

enough, there was his ball on the floor of the comfortless dungeon. As he picked it up he turned round and saw a woman ascending the circular stairs. Being above him he could only see her skirt which was long and covered her feet. She disappeared upwards and Chips thought nothing of it until he got to the gate; then he warned the custodian that there was a lady still in the castle. But the custodian replied that there was no one there, and indeed this proved to be the case. Slowly it dawned on Chips that he had seen the ghost of the white lady who is said to haunt that tower. He remembers that he heard no sound from her footsteps and described the skirt as not showing any colour in the twilight of the tower.

(12) My final story from the present century is told by the late Elliott O'Donnell in "Screaming Skulls and other Ghost Stories". He relates how at the International Club for Psychical Research in 1913 a Mr. Taylor related a story told to him by Mrs. King of Torquay. She stated that her brother, who was an officer in the Army, went, whilst on leave, to see Berry Pomeroy Castle. Whilst wandering over the ruins he saw a young and beautiful girl beckoning to him from the summit of one of the lofty, ivy-clad walls. She was wearing a somewhat quaint though becoming costume. He, supposing that she was afraid to move lest she should fall, hastened to find a way to reach her. Having begun to climb up to her, he had almost reached her when the masonry beneath his feet gave way, and it was only by a miracle that he managed to save himself from falling headlong to a considerable depth. Clinging desperately to a narrow ledge he was, luckily for himself, eventually seen and rescued. But on mentioning the plight of the lovely damsel he was told that there was no reason to concern himself about her; she was not of this world, but the much dreaded phantom of a long defunct member of the Pomeroy family, who took a fiendish delight in luring people, especially men, to their destruction.

Turning now from the stories related in the twentieth century we will next consider the well known experience of Dr., later Sir Walter Farquhar. He was a royal physician and created a baronet in 1796. Quoting from "Annals", Note 98, p.443, the writer, after telling how he was summoned one day on a professional visit to the castle from Torquay, relates:- "Although a ruin, there still remained two or three rooms in which the steward resided with his wife. It was the latter who was ill. On the doctor's arrival he was asked to remain in the outer apartment while the steward went to see if his wife was prepared. 'This apartment was large and ill-proportioned; around it ran richly carved panels of oak that age had changed to the hue of ebony. The only light in the room was admitted through the chequered panes of a gorgeously stained window, in which were emblazoned the arms of the former Lords of Berry Pomeroy. In one corner to the right of the wide fireplace was a flight of dark oaken steps, forming part of a staircase leading apparently to some chamber above.' Whilst the doctor was waiting the door opened, and a richly dressed lady entered the room. The doctor, thinking it was some visitor, rose and made a step forward, but the lady paid no attention to him, and hurried across the room, wringing her hands, and evidently in the greatest distress. Arriving at the foot of the stairs, she paused a moment and then hurried up them. As she reached the highest stair the light fell strongly on her features, and displayed a young and beautiful countenance, but, to use the doctor's own words 'if ever human face exhibited agony and remorse; if ever eye, that index of the soul, portrayed anguish uncheered by hope, and suffering without interval; if ever features betrayed that within the wearer's bosom there dwelt a hell, those features and that being were then present to me'.

"Almost immediately afterwards he was called to see the patient, whom he found so ill that he had to give his undivided attention to her case. The next day, however, finding her much better, he inquired of the steward as to the lady he had seen, and described her appearance. The steward became greatly agitated, exclaiming repeatedly 'My poor wife!' But eventually, becoming calmer, he told the doctor that he was sure that she would now die, and enlightened him as to the history of the apparition so far as he knew it. It appears that it was the daughter of a former baron of Berry Pomeroy, who had borne a child to her own father and strangled it in the room above. He added that he had lived at the castle for 30 years, and had never known the omen fail, and that it had last been seen the day his son was drowned. Although the doctor considered his patient much better and pronounced that all danger was over, the omen had been no mistake and the poor woman died that day.

"Many years afterwards Sir Walter was called upon by a lady who came to consult him about her sister who was suffering from severe shock. She explained that during the summer she had accompanied her brother and sister to Torquay, whence they had driven over one morning to inspect the ruins of Berry Pomeroy. The steward they found was ill, and there was some difficulty about getting the keys. She herself and her brother had, therefore, gone in search of them, leaving their sister in a large outer room (apparently, from her description, the same as that in which the doctor had before been put). When they returned they found their sister in a terrible state of alarm and distress, declaring that she had seen an apparition (the description of which tallied exactly with that formerly seen by Sir Walter). They had endeavoured to rally her out of it by expressing their disbelief and laughing at her fear; but their sister only grew worse and her state now occasioned them the greatest alarm. In reply to a question of Sir Walter's she said that the steward had died whilst they were still at the castle. The doctor then said 'Madam, I will make a point of seeing your sister immediately, but it is no delusion. This I think it most proper to state most positively before any interview. I, myself, saw the same figure under somewhat similar circumstances, and about the same hour of the day: I should decidedly oppose any raillery or incredulity being expressed on the subject in your sister's presence.' The lady recovered and the apparition was never seen again for the old steward was the last person to inhabit the castle."

(A full account of this story is given in "Haunted Homes and Family Legends" by J. H. Ingram.)

The above is one of the traditional hauntings of Berry—the woman is usually described as dressed in blue and always very beautiful. She was clearly the apparition that the clergyman's daughter saw recently, for she described the colour of her dress. She was probably the one which the army officer tried to rescue, although the colour of her attire is not mentioned in that story.

The next most persistent ghost is that of the Lady Margaret, who was imprisoned by her sister, Eleanor. She appears in white and is seen on the rampart walk near St. Margaret's Tower. Her appearance is said to betoken death to the beholder. Although supposed to have been seen within the last twenty years by a medium I can give no definite instance of her appearance. Another of the old ghost stories concerns the two lovers described in the chapter on Folklore who were stabbed to death by the lady's brother. They are said to be seen beckoning to each other across an abyss which neither can cross. The lady in blue is also said to be seen in the woods.

The last of the older stories concerns that Pomeroy of olden times who appears with a hawk on his wrist and holding a silver spur. He, like Lady Margaret, foretells the death of the beholder. You may read of his appearances in Mrs. Bray's "Sir Henry de Pomeroy". He may, of course have been entirely her creation, for I do not find a mention of him elsewhere.

In summing up the evidence of the stories collected in this chapter, it seems to me that both sceptics and believers have quite unexpectedly been witnesses of things which they never thought to see. Mr. Ellis is among the former class, yet he affirms (1) and (2). Mrs. Charlesworth, on the other hand, was psychically sensitive and in (9) she could see a man whom the children could not. The first eleven stories are vouched for by unimpeachable witnesses. No. 12 took place over 80 years ago now, but it would never have been told to so august a body as the International Club for Psychical Research unless the narrator could at that time have produced the victim who was ensnared by the lady in blue into climbing a dangerous wall. Sir Walter Farquhar's double story is also past suspicion, and with its hint of the lady in blue being often seen in the past takes us back to the middle of the eighteenth century. I wish that I could produce evidence of a sighting of Lady Margaret in recent times. It is, however, rather a grim thought that since she presages an early death to the beholder there would of course never be anyone alive to tell us of their experience!

Section of Park Wall

CHAPTER 6

The Deer Parks

Most people visit Berry Pomeroy without grasping the fact that the castle stands in a former deer park of over 340 acres in extent which has an impressive free stone wall completely enclosing it. As the visitor stands facing the Lodge Gate he will see on his left a short lane. At the end of it is an old shippen with a steep pitch to its roof of red tiles. From this vantage point a good view is obtained of the Park Wall which begins at the barn and continues downhill in a roughly WNW direction. An even better view is from the point where the road from the village forks left to the Castle. From the gateway near here the wall will be seen going across country in a straight line, and its importance when compared with other field boundaries is immediately apparent. After about three quarters of a mile the wall turns a little E of N and descends to the Gatcombe valley, where it crosses the brook at Netherton, climbing the hill beyond almost in a straight line. After half a mile it alters course to the E and after another half mile reaches a point known as Park Corner. Thence it goes to Broom Park Barn and soon proceeds in a straight line to the Gatcombe Brook once more, which it now reaches at the pond below the Castle. It reappears by the stile on the other side of the lane and goes back to the Castle Lodge in a SW direction. The total length of the wall is roughly 2.7 miles. Throughout its length it is complete, and apart from intruding gateways, forms an unbroken stretch of free stone walling of a very superior style.

The wall averages 8ft. in height, although there are sections which must approach 10ft. Again in places where time has destroyed it the height is down to 4ft. Its width is very uniform at 2ft.8in. The downhill approach to the Gatcombe Brook at Netherton is a particularly well preserved section, probably on account of its less exposed position in the valley. There must at one time have been coping stones throughout the entire length of the wall. Understandably there are now long stretches where they are missing. It is strange to notice how the coping stones, where they still remain, seem to attract a thick growth of ivy, which in its turn tends to bring them down and so destroys the top of the wall. The stone used is the local limestone which will have been quarried in abundance nearby. The stone has weathered to an attractive pinkish-grey hue. There is much lichen on the shady side. Where rebuilding has taken place it has been done well, but with no real attempt to copy the original. A characteristic of the wall is the size of the stones, none of which exceed about 2ft. in length. Many have been roughly shaped to hold them in position. Very small, almost wafer-like stones have been purposely shaped to hold the big stones in position and to pack the gaps which, in a Dartmoor free stone wall, for instance, would have been left as they were.

A pleasing feature is the treatment of gateways where they occur. Here no attempt at gateposts has been made, but the wall itself, on either side, has been beautifully rounded off. In the valley below the Castle the wall has been much rebuilt and its salient characteristics are lost for a while. The purpose of the wall was of course to enclose a deer park. The Survey of 1292 says that it was 300 acres in extent, this being the first reference to it so far noticed. Polwhele, writing in 1797 considers that the wall enclosed 500 acres, which was an exaggeration. Worthy (T.D.A. 1915) gives the figure as 340 acres, whilst my calculations bring it to 341 acres. So these latter figures almost agree. Worthy also says that a quarter of the length of the wall had been overthrown by tree trunks; this has now been made good. Lysons, writing in 1822, on P.43 states laconically "There is a deer park at Berry Pomeroy".

I have been in touch with Laurence Garner, the Secretary of the Dry Stone Walling Association. Although no one from the Association has been able to inspect the wall so far, he feels from the description that it is the sort of work undertaken in the 18th century.* It is such a fine piece of craftsmanship that one might have hoped to find records and accounts with regard to its building. Unfortunately nothing of the kind exists among the Somerset Papers at the Wiltshire Record Office at Trowbridge. If the present wall is of 18th century origin, then it would be in all probability the second wall to enclose the Park, for at Trowbridge there is an Inquisitio Post Mortem on the death of Sir Edward Seymour which mentions it. A translation from the Latin original speaks of ". . . one Barton and messuage called or known as the Barton or House of Bury and

---

*Donn's map of 1765 shows the park boundaries exactly as they are today. This does not prove that the present wall was there, however.

one park called the Parke of Berry Pomeroy. There were formerly two parks in Berry Pomeroy". Later there is mention of the "castle, park and parks of Bury Pomeroy". Several times the phrase "the aforesaid mansion, house, castle and park lands" occurs.

No difficulty arises over the mention of an older Park, for this first Park was mentioned as early as 1207, when Henry de la Pomerai (4) was granted official permission by King John (Pipe Rolls) to enclose 100 acres for the purpose of a deer park; for this he paid 10 marks. The earlier Park is mentioned again in the Survey of 1292 when it is described as "overdone with wild beasts". Where was this older Park? We should be wrong if we thought that it was contained in the later one, for we have the testimony of the Inquisition that there were two parks. A point to notice in passing is the fact that the Castle site could not have been in the old park, for it is the later park which encloses it. Is this perhaps yet another proof that in 1207 there was as yet no castle around which to make a deer park? It is sad to record that no possible site for the old park has as yet come to light. The Tithe Map does not help with field names, and no walls or banks enclosing as much as 100 acres have been noticed. One fact is clear, however, the early park must have enclosed land where there was ample water for the requirements of the herds. The manor has only one really active stream to show and this is the Gatcombe Brook. Unless dew ponds or artificially made ponds existed in the west part of the manor at one time, then I would be inclined to suggest that the park could have fitted into an area on both sides of brook at Netherton, between the present park wall and the Little Hempston boundary. This is conjecture, however, and no more, for there are no old banks or tumbled walls to be seen at Netherton. As against this theory we must not forget old John Hooker (see p. 133) who refers to stones which "do growe in the East syde of the Ryver Darte in Berry pomeroy pk". Did Hooker, writing in 1599 mean what we do by the word "park"? Once again no enclosing banks of this 100 acre park are to be found near the river now. It is a pleasant enough spot to raise deer, but more one cannot say.

Whilst it was a common thing for country estates to be enclosed by imposing walls, yet it was by no means common for a mere deer park wall to be maintained when there was an absentee landlord. The Castle was inhabited until c.1688, yet we are asked to believe that a splendid new wall was undertaken in the 18th century when no one resided at the Castle. The value of a herd of deer must have been far exceeded by the outlay for building and maintaining this expensive wall. Eventually, of course, the herds of deer were no longer maintained and the land reverted to agricultural use. The wall would then become of use as field boundaries, and for this reason it still stands today. All the same the Park wall adds yet one other unanswered question to the story of Berry Pomeroy. Why was this fine wall rebuilt and maintained so well?

Yet another intriguing question is posed by an entry in the "Annals" (p.290) where the writer quotes from a paper of the 11th Duke dated 1664. He says "There was in addition a mansion house in the park of Berry Pomeroy, and a capital house, farm, barton, etc., probably the same that remains near the church". Where was the "mansion house" and what purpose did it serve? One can find no signs of any ruined house in the park today, but that is not to say that it is not there for the finding—however scanty the remains may be. Only two lanes actually lead into the park now. One is a little over half a mile from the village on the road to Little Hempston. Here a right fork climbs up to a gate in the park wall. On the left, a few yards below it, and towards the valley below is a tumbled mass of stones, looking rather like an old quarry. Could this be the site of the mansion of 1664? Trees surround the site which could be evidence of former occupation. I have seen several such places which are known to be the remains of old homesteads. As against this not a trickle of water is apparent anywhere.

The other lane which enters the Park is on the opposite side and leads up to it from Afton. It ends after about half a mile, although old maps mark it as continuing to Shadrack; but this latter section has now quite disappeared. The end of the lane is marked on the Tithe Map as "Park Corner", whilst a small enclosure beside the wall is "Park Corner Orchard" of which not a vestige now remains. On the left is a gate through which a definite track proceeds in a direction roughly SE. Soon to the left of the wall, a barn is to be seen. This is "Broom Park Barn". It is old, constructed of stone and cob and with a steep-pitched roof. The lane soon peters out beside a heap of uneven mounds—once again a possible site for an old homestead. A cup-shaped hollow by the mounds could be a wellhead. So this is a more promising site than the former. Here we have the remembrance of an orchard and an old shippen—so often all that is left standing of a former holding—and a probable water supply. So apart from these two sites I can offer no others. What may once have stood in the dark plantation on Summer Hill no one can say. To what use was this former mansion put? A dower house perhaps?

Finally, still in the park, and on the warm southern slopes to the SW of the Castle, the old field names of Great Orchard, Little Orchard, Brake Orchard, Plum Garden and Castle Garden show how the old cultivation lay just below the castle for whose needs it provided.

In 1413 there is a record of two men who were probably keepers—John de la Park and Robert at Park.

Kitchen Block

CHAPTER 7

Documents and Letters

When the first Duke of Somerset purchased the manor and castle from Sir Thomas Pomerey in 1548, he stipulated that every document concerning them should be handed over. This was done, and as a result the present Duke, the 18th to bear the title, has been able to deposit in the Wiltshire County Record Office at Trowbridge a wonderful collection of no less than 339 charters concerning the Pomeroy period of ownership. They were, happily for us, arranged and calendared in 1925 by the late John Scanes. Each document is recorded with regard to its subject matter and date upon two large sheets of cartridge paper. The dates range from 1190 to 1547. There are a few extra documents which concern business arising from the sale of the manor. Scanes was a school master at Maiden Bradley, Wilts., where the Duke of Somerset has his seat. It was fortunate for posterity that he had a knowledge of Latin, for it would seem that he was the first over the centuries to take a real interest in the charters. They consist entirely of deeds in connection with the manor and are for the most part leases. One day it is to be hoped that someone will undertake a history of the manor. Certainly they will not lack for data, since the Seymour period of ownership is just as rich in documentation. For the writer the sad thing was to find that this mass of written words contains very little which is relevant to this book. They tell us nothing of the building, maintenance, expenses or extension of the castle.

A few charters of course are of value because they tell us something about particular members of the Pomeroy family. For instance there is a very important confirmation made to Henry de la Pomerai (2) of the possession of his lands both in England and Normandy. It was given by King Richard I in 1193/4. All who have commented on this charter so far have mis-read it, stating that the confirmation was made to Henry (3) and his son. This is not what the Latin says, however. The translation is an affirmation "to our well-beloved and faithful knight, Henry de Pomeraio, otherwise Henry the son and his heirs etc." Now it is recorded that Henry (2), being the second to hold that name, was known by the soubriquet "Henry the son" and this is exactly what the third line of the charter (included here) says. The implication of the charter is therefore far-reaching, for it shows that Henry (2) was actually pardoned by the King for his rebellion, and on payment of a large fine all his lands were restored in the last year of his life. So the story of his suicide, either by being bled to death or by leaping over the precipice at Berry would appear by the correct understanding of this charter to be untrue—always supposing that the King's pardon reached him in time. A witness of the charter was one William of St. Marychurch. So this son of Devon had raised himself to be a part of the King's entourage. Whilst Henry (2)'s rebellion appears to have been pardoned for some reason, yet the fine of 700 marks was to embarass the Pomeroy estate for years to come.

The remarkable Survey of 1292 has already been discussed. It is mentioned again here because of its great value as a mine of information about the manor of Berry in the 13th century. It is discussed at length by Powley in "The House of de la Pomerai" and there is also an able article upon it by Reichel in T.D.A. vol.28.

But the really outstanding document with regard to the castle itself is the Grant to John Sapcotes of the keeping of the lands of Sir Richard Pomeray in 1497 (pat. Rolls 1494-1509, 108). It was given because of the minority of his son Edward after his death. In it we are told of the third share which Sir Richard left to his widow, Lady

King Richard I's confirmation to Henry de la Pomerai (II) of his lands in England and Normandy

Elizabeth, both in the manor and in the castle and manor house. The fascinating list of rooms which were allotted to her has been already discussed in the opening chapter.

The most active member of the family from a legal viewpoint was John de la Pomerai (c.1352-1416), for between the years 1374 and 1413 he issued no fewer than 61 grants of one kind or another. The leases include even the manor itself which he leased on quite a few occasions. If it was truly he who built the gatehouse and curtain wall then it is possible he needed ready money with which to do it.

It had up to now been thought that the first mention of a "Castle" at Berry was in the settlement of the property after the death of Sir Richard Pomeray in 1497, but there is among the Pomeroy papers a lease of "a certain mylle with its leat called castell mylle". This is dated 1467 and will refer to the old mill below the castle which still stands today. It seems an absurdly late date for the first reference on paper to the castle. Perhaps the lack of any mention proves that John Pomeroy's meagre fortifications did not impress his neighbours. It was to be two or three generations before the courtesy title of "Castle" was applied to the buildings.

The final lengthy charters concerning the sale of Berry Pomeroy to the Duke of Somerset in 1547/8 refer to the latter in extremely grandiose terms. He is referred to as "the high and mighty Prince Edward, Duke of Somerset, Viscount Beauchamp, Erle of Hertford, lord Seymour of the honourable order of the Garter, knight, Erle Marshall of England and High Treasurer of the same, oldest uncle to the King's highness and Guardian of his Majestie's most royall Person and Protector of all his highnes Realmes, Dominations and Subjects".

With the advent of the Seymours our castle firmly turned its back on the Middle Ages and all that they stood for. Its successive owners became much involved in the stirring events of the times. There were first the alarms of the Spanish Armada and at the close of the 16th century a further threat of a Spanish invasion. After a lull came the Civil War when the castle was at the centre of much Royalist intrigue. Then came the overthrow of King James II, and finally the landing of William of Orange at Brixham. In all these great happenings the Seymours at Berry Castle were closely involved, and a great deal of their correspondence survives.

In the "Annals" (Appendices I & J, pp.490-504) are a series of letters from the Earl of Bath to the first Baronet (grandson of the Lord

Protector) respecting the defence of the south-west against the threatened Spanish invasion. They begin in 1595. The Earl usually begins "Good Cousin Seymour". There are return letters from the Baronet at Berry Castle, and others of the series concern the Mayor of Dartmouth, Justices, Constable etc. Of greater interest, however, is the correspondence of the 3rd Baronet, for this deals with the exciting events of the Civil War when he was Governor of Dartmouth Castle. There are letters to Sir Edward from King Charles I, Prince Maurice, Lord Bath and others. Some are in the Devon County Record Office at Exeter and others will be found in the "Annals" (Appendix L, pp.510-516). One, which is at Exeter, (1392n/L1644/45) was of such urgent importance in its day that we quote it here:-

Address:
ffor Colenell Seamore
Governour at Dartmouth
haste post haste
. . . this letter per posted and passd
Maurice.

S^r I have been lately informed by Sr John Berkely of an Insurrection about or near to Torbay for suppression whereof I shall recomend it you & Colonell Carey to whom I have writt purposely about yt I shall desire your speedy   in this business and to give mee an Accompt thereof, Hnd. Sir I rest
              Sir your af. friend
                 Maurice

I send you here inclosed a warrt. for the   of this service.
Oakhampton
11 July
   8 in the morning   Gr. of Dartmouth

After the Restoration when Sir Edward, now ageing, was much in London owing to his duties as Member of Parliament, he wrote some excellent, gossipy letters to his wife, the Lady Anne Seymour at Berry. They bring us very close to this particular Sir Edward and are to be found in Chapter 3 under the heading of the 3rd Baronet.

Many letters from the famous 4th Baronet, the Speaker of the House of Commons, are to be read in the "Annals", but they are outside our period in relation to the story of the castle up to the time of its desertion and demolition.

To sum up, the written word concerning Berry and the men who owned it is of very great value. The Pomeroy charters on the one hand are splendid examples of the kind of legal procedure adopted in the administration of a manor from 1190-1548. On the other hand the great value of the Seymour period lies in the surviving letters which tell us so much of the important historical events which took place around the castle in the 16th and 17th centuries.

Stairs from courtyard to rampart

Looking into Great Parlour

CHAPTER 8
Early References, Books and Poems

The earliest writer to mention the Castle is John Leland who wrote his "Itinerary" between 1534 and 1543. He states that "Byri Pomerey Town lyith hard by the Est Ende of Totenes Bridge, Byry Pomerey Chirch almost a mile of and Byry Pomerey Castelle about half a Mile from the Chirch". So this account, though terse, is valuable because it was made by one who must have been the very first sightseer. It is interesting also to notice in passing that Leland wrote before the property passed from the hands of the Pomeroys. The "castelle" had yet a few more years in the care of the family who built it.

The next visitor to Berry was John Hooker (1505-1601). In his "Synopsis Chorographical" he wrote "bysydes that of late in the yeare 1599 iii special stones very fayre beautyfull and of estimcon whereof too do growe in the East syde of the Ryver Darte in Berry pomeroy pk. Theon of theym is of dunneshe of Many coullor intermixt with blewe and greene coullor and having a very fayre vaynes in it of whyte coullor wch being pullyshed is compted to be purphure as good as any can be. And of the scoples or stones thereof the castle of berry is ptly builded".

The next writers were three who all wrote in the third decade of the 17th century—Westcote, Pole and Risdon. Their account of the Castle therefore comes about a century after Leland's and they all wrote in the Seymour period of ownership. Tristram Risdon's account is not long and may be quoted in full. It was written in 1630 and was included in his "Chorographical Description or Survey of the County of Devon" p.156. "This manor of Bery was held by Ralf de Pomerai in the Conqueror's time, unto whom he gave much land in this county, where he built his castle, and seated himself, which is an ancient honour, and his posterity were barons of Bery, which land they enjoyed and dwelt there unto the reign of King Edward 6th and their name now remaineth, though not in that honour their ancestors lived in, and will be perpetuated to posterity by the places in this county bearing their adjunct. This was sold by Sir Thomas Pomerai unto Edward Seymour, Duke of Somerset, whose eldest son, the lord Edward Seymour, dwelt there; whose son, Sir Edward

Seymour, Knight and baronet, made it a very stately house, which his (sic) the seat of Sir Edward Seymour, Knight and baronet, his son. The name I find to be very ancient, for in the time of King Hengist the Saxon, who confederated with the Scots against Aurelius Ambrosius, he was taken prisoner by Edulph Seimer, a noble Briton". Note that Risdon says that Lord Seymour dwelt at Berry, but that it was his son who made it "a very stately house". He then goes on to say, in the present tense, that it is the seat of Sir Edward Seymour, Knight and baronet, his son. This evidence is valuable for it confutes the story repeated by some that the Seymours never actually lived in the grand new portion of the house which they built. Risdon was living in 1630 and thus testifies that in his day the Lord Protector's great-grandson resided at the Castle, "in a very stately house".

Thomas Westcote, Gent., finished his "A View of Devonshire in MDCXXX with a pedigree of Most of its Gentry" in the year mentioned, but it was not published until 1845. The reference to Berry Pomeroy is concerned entirely with geneaology, but his descriptions of the Pomeroy and Seymour tombs in the Parish Church are excellent:- "In this church some of them (the Seymours) are interred and also of the Pomeroys and the windows beautified with armories. As for the monuments there are but two of them of more than ordinary remark, the one in the north wall of the chancel erected to the memory of Sir Richard Pomeroy and his lady; being an altar-piece laid over with a fair serpentine stone (which had been inlaid with divers coats of arms and mottos in copper gilded) now embezzled or worn away by time; at the E end of which is Pomeroy impaled with Denzil; and at the W end Pomeroy's coat single done in stone or plaster.

"In the N aisle is a noble monument erected to the memory of the Seymours, where lie, piled one over another, the bodies of the Lord Edward Seymour (the first of this family that resided in this county), his son Sir Edward Seymour, bart, with his lady, a daughter of Champernon of Dartington; under which is cut in stone also the proportions of 11 children.

"In a fair marble table, in the middle of the monument, is this inscription, 'Here lie the bodies of the hon. the Lord Edward Seymour, Kt, son unto the Rt. Hon. Edward Seymour, who died 2nd May, 1593. Also of Edward Seymour, his son, bart, who died 10th April, 1613; and the Lady Elizabeth his wife, daughter of Sir Arthur

Champernon, who had issue by him, the said Sir Edward Seymour, bart, eleven children'."

He also describes "armories" in the church windows visible in 1696 (1626?):- Montague or Montacute, Botreaux, Merton, Stafford, Courtenay, St. George, Pomeroy, Raleigh, Denzil, Filleigh, Esse or Ash, Hillersdon, Trevillian, Pomeroy, Beauchamp, Dowman, Aston, Pomeroy. England and France. Pomeroy, Dennis, of Combe Rawleigh, Pomeroy.

Sir William Pole's "Collections towards a Description of the County of Devon" was undertaken before 1635—the year of his death. Like Westcote's book it was not published until much later—in this case 1791. Pole was obsessed with family pedigrees, and in the case of Berry Pomeroy nothing else is mentioned. A comparison between his family tree of the Pomeroys with Powley's, undertaken over three centuries later, is certainly of interest.

Next in the succession of old writers comes The Reverend John Prince, for so many years the respected vicar of the parish. Writing in 1702 his account of the families of Pomeroy and Seymour, like Pole's, consists entirely of pedigrees and need not concern us. His graphic account of the Castle at the height of its fame, however, is of great value; it has already been quoted (p. 41).

In the 18th century there is first W. G. Maton, who between 1704 and 1706 wrote "Observations of the Western Counties of England". His style is florid, but he does describe the Castle which shows us how it appeared to visitors in his day. We may be faintly amused at his concern for the safety of the fabric which has survived a further two centuries since his day. He writes:- "Berry Pomeroy is not more than a mile from Totnes. The great gate (with the walls of the south front), the north wing of the court, or quadrangle, some apartments on the W side and a turret or two are the principal remains of the building, and they are so finely overhung with the branches of trees and shrubs that grow close to the walls, so beautifully mantled with ivy, and so richly encrusted with moss, that they constitute the most picturesque objects that can be imagined . . . The eastern tower is accessible by a passage from the room over the gateway; there we found was the best part for surveying the environs of the castle. The interior part appears to be considerably more modern than the gate and on the walls, the windows being square or oblong, with linterns and crossbars of stone. It is going rapidly to decay, however, and the walls being composed of slate might be entirely demolished with little trouble. When perfect these apartments must have been extremely grand, and were decorated in a splendid manner if one might judge from the mouldings, columns etc. which remain. The large room over the gateway is divided by a wall supported by three pillars and circular arches, but it is not easy to discover the use of it. There was evidently a portcullis to the gate, which is turreted and embattled, and over it the arms of the family of Pomeroy are still to be seen."

At the end of the 18th century the Reverend Richard Polwhele's "History of Devonshire" appeared in three volumes (1793-1806). He mentions our castle on p.491, quoting extensively from Prince. He concludes "The ruins of the castle are an object of great curiosity to travellers. The north view seems most romantic, from the old fragments of the castle breaking thro' the deep umbrage of the fantastic woods. The stone wall is still traceable round the park of about 500 acres".

In 1819 there appeared W. Dugdale's "The New British Traveller" (Devonshire). On p.108 is a further florid account of the castle and its surroundings. He extensively quotes Prince and Maton, but adds nothing to what had already been written. His final sentence, however, is to be noted for he writes "In the wars between Charles I and Parliament, this castle was dismantled". It is strange how the earlier writers, Prince, Maton and Polwhele never mention any such thing. Mrs. Bray does, however; she also wrote in the early 19th century. This rather bears out my theory, mentioned elsewhere, that this is a legend which gained credence at that period but is not mentioned in the previous century which of course was not so far from the days of the Civil War.

Finally, among the earlier writers, comes the Reverend Daniel Lysons, who in 1822 published the 6th volume of his "Magna Britannia—a Topographical and Historical Account of Devonshire". On p.436 appears a short account of the Castle. He mentions that the Pomeroy arms were "not many years ago" to be seen over gateway. So by that time they had finally weathered away.

Turning now to poems and novels, we have already in the chapter on Folklore quoted from the only fragments available of Mrs. Cuming's poems on Berry Pomeroy. But there is one work worthy of mention also, it is "Berry Pomeroy"—a poem by Luke M. Combes which was first published in Torquay by private subscription in

1872. It was in two volumes consisting in all of three cantos. The story of the poem concerns Sir Ralph de Pomeroy who sets out to join King Richard I at Dartmouth, whence he was to sail on the Third Crusade. This was in 1190. With him were Sir Guy de Champernowne, Walter de Totneis and de la Pole. Sir Ralph's neice, the Lady Margaret Pomeroy, is the heiress of many manors, but the Church tries to influence her to go into a Convent when her wealth would automatically be made over to the Church. A disguised pilgrim overhears plans about this being made secretly at Torre Abbey. He then makes his way to Compton Castle by way of an underground passage. At the same time Sir Ralph's wife, the Lady Marion, suddely dies and Margaret is unprotected. She is told that her uncle is slain and that her father, who has been abroad for ten years, is also dead. She is then asked by Sir Hugh Trehane to marry him, but she spurns his offer because she loves de la Pole. So Sir Hugh goes off to the Crusade. Meanwhile the pilgrim goes to the castle and tells Lady Margaret that although her uncle is dead, yet her father is still living. He warns her of her peril and gives her a dagger.

He next goes to Torre Abbey where, in a secret room, he overhears a meeting of the Abbot with the Abbot of Buckfast and the Prior of Modbury. They plan to abduct Margaret. Soon Sir Anselm returns to Berry only to find that Margaret has indeed been abducted and her faithful hound, Damon, who tried to defend her, has been killed. He goes to Torre Abbey and searches it in vain. After a year has elapsed and de la Pole and Trehane have returned from the Crusade, a monk betrays the Abbot. They follow a secret passage from Berry Pomeroy which leads towards Torre; in it they find a cell where Margaret is imprisoned. She has been starved and is at death's door, but is nursed back to health, however, and marries her lover.

Whether the whole story is pure fiction or whether Combes was told it by someone living in the district we cannot tell. Torre Abbey was not founded until 1196. Sir Ralph and Sir Anselm Pomeroy are not known to history, so the story is most certainly not founded on fact.

"Henry de Pomeroy or the Eve of St. John" by Mrs. Bray begins with the description of a visit to the castle made in 1838. She writes thus:- "My companion had visited it many years before, but now scarcely recognised it again, so much had it altered by the course of time . . . I do not wonder that he found some difficulty in recognising an old acquaintance here, for the very gateway of the castle was so hidden by trees, and so overgrown with ivy, that on first approach it is no easy matter to make out what it is." A little girl appears who acts as guide; she continues:- "Passing under the gateway, we ascended to what is generally called the chapel; but which was evidently the Guardroom above the entrance, as the opening for the fall of the portcullis still remains in the walls". She goes on to say that all this is "most likely the work of that de Pomeroy on whom the manor was bestowed by William the Conqueror and who was the original founder of the castle.

"When Henry III ascended the throne he took the castle from the Baron la Zouche, on account of his having espoused the cause of Richard III and bestowed it on that celebrated knight, Sir Piers Edgcumbe, who had rendered him essential services when he was Earl of Richmond and only a Pretender to the crown.*

"That the gateway and the most ancient portions of Berry Pomeroy are of Norman construction I do not doubt. That something was added to the castle by the celebrated Sir Henry de Pomeroy who figured in the reign of Richard I is very likely: that La Zouche also repaired and made additions to it is more than probable: but the whole of the interior building, the palace (for so it might be called) was the work of Sir Piers Edgcumbe, admits, I think, of no question, as it has none of the florid decoration, none of the mixture of Grecian and Gothic, which we may see in similar works of the time of Henry VIII and still more so in the heavy and ungraceful architecture of the reign of Elizabeth.

"After a careful survey of the whole, we could not help saying that Berry Pomeroy would be a most interesting ruin, if it were not so encumbered with brambles and trees, as in many places you can see nothing else. That portion of the castle which is stationed on the esplanade, above a rocky precipice at the back of the building is so completely surrounded by trees that you are scarcely conscious you are near a precipice till on its very verge.

She continues "The same intelligent little person added 'And that is the place where the castle was taken in the time of Charles I. They took it by guns—great guns planted on yonder hill' . . . as for the purpose of strengthening the building and also for securing it

---

*Here she seems to be confusing Berry Pomeroy with Totnes Castle.

against the inspection of visitors, walls with rude embattlements have recently been built from one part of the structure to another, giving it a patchwork appearance incompatible with picturesque beauty."

As this is the only comprehensive 19th century description of the castle which is preserved it is of considerable value to us today. It also shows how little was known of the ownership of the castle through the centuries, and how easy it was to draw quite wrong conclusions as to the age of the building when all details were obscured by vegetation.

Turning now to the novel itself, its title shows that the hero is Henry (2) de la Pomerai. The book was first published in 1841 and is the earliest of the known novels. It demonstrates admirably the aura of folklore and romance which surrounded Berry Castle at that time. The action takes place first at Tavistock Abbey, then at St. Michael's Mount and finally at the Castle. The gist of the story is that a Lady Adela is, against her will, taken to the Convent at St. Michael's Mount where she is to become a nun. Sir Henry, who loves her, rides after her, captures the Mount in the name of Prince John, and is just about to marry her in the castle chapel when his men warn him that armed men of King Richard's party are surrounding them. Seizing Lady Adela, Sir Henry rides with her in a desperate dash for the shore; but the incoming tide engulfs them. His bride-to-be is drowned, but the distraught Sir Henry escapes to Berry Pomeroy. Soon a Herald from the King arrives and Sir Henry entertains him for a while. The story then follows the folklore, for after a day or so the Herald produces a Warrant for Sir Henry's arrest. The latter, in a rage, produces a dagger and stabs the Herald to death. Realising that all is now lost, he blindfolds his charger, mounts it and gallops along the north terrace, leaping over the precipice at the end in a headlong fall to his death. So ends the book. The style is verbose and rather akin to that of Sir Walter Scott. It moves well to its conclusion, however; the description of the race for shore and Sir Henry's mad deathleap are really gripping, and worth all the rest of the book put together.

The novel demonstrates how well the authoress was acquainted with the folklore which still survives today. Whether the ghostly appearance of a former Pomeroy who augured death was a figment of her imagination or whether it was a legend alive in her day we cannot tell. I certainly have not read it elsewhere.

Mrs. Henry Wood, the well known authoress of "East Lynne", published "Pomeroy Abbey" in 1878. A further edition in 1898 records a printing of 48,000 copies and demonstrates the amazing popularity of this writer. Mrs. Wood must have visited Berry Castle and been more impressed by the wonders of the Pomeroys, as related in folklore, than in the Castle. She wanted to write a novel about the family, but in a nineteenth century setting. So with their ancestral home in ruins she had no alternative but to transport them lock, stock and barrel to a mansion by the sea which she calls "Pomeroy Abbey". This was a thriving Victorian country house, but dating in part from mediaeval times. Here the family are shown living in right royal style with an army of retainers. The head of the house is "The Pomeroy" and his wife "The Lady of Pomeroy". Apart from the name and Pomeroy tradition this novel has nothing to do with Berry Pomeroy Castle.

"The House of de la Pomerai" by Edward B. Powley, B.A.(Lond.), M.A.(Liverpool), B.Litt.(Oxon), F.R.Hist.S., was published by the University of Liverpool, Hodder and Stoughton, London, 1947, only about 250 copies being printed. This is undoubtedly THE book on the Pomeroy family, and it is improbable that anything on so scholarly a level will be undertaken again. Years of research and devotion must have gone into the making of such a wonderful book. Its excellent production and the luxurious paper upon which it is printed make it a pleasure to handle. The author provides pedigrees of the Pomeroys, and traces the doings of each generation of the owners of Berry from the Conquest to the year 1548, when the sale of the manor and castle to the Lord Protector took place. He does more than this, however, for collaterals and American offshoots are also dealt with. The compiling of the footnotes, references and indexes alone must have been a formidable task; but all has been undertaken with consummate skill. From this book we learn a great deal about the house of de la Pomerai, but not so much about the castle; for whoever writes on that subject is beset with immediate difficulties through lack of documentation, the abundance of which enabled Powley to write so authoritatively about the Pomeroys. Their doings through the centuries are vouched for on all sides, but not so their castle.

As the reader would expect from the title the bulk of the book deals with the family itself, but the author very sensibly gives also a brief account of the generations of the Seymours who lived at Berry.

This was almost a necessity if the ruins in their present form are to be understood. The chapter on the castle itself has been undertaken with caution—indeed the reader is often asked the leading questions, and there are some shrewd omissions of opinion. In 1947, when the book was published, the buildings were still mantled in ivy and much that is obvious now simply could not be seen then. It is difficult to be as enthusiastic as Powley was over the strategic strength of the castle site. Here the experienced historian for once allows himself to romance.

The style of the book is for the scholar rather than the casual reader, but no one attempting a serious study of the castle and the two families which occupied it can get on without it; the present writer has been driven back to it again and again, and freely admits that the chapter in the present book about the Pomeroys could not have been undertaken without the solid and dependable background to the historical Pomeroys which Powley provides. Never once do we get lead astray by the legendary greatness of the family. All is solid fact backed up by the weight of indisputable documentation.

"The Castle of Berry Pomeroy" by Edward Montague must have been first printed about the middle of the nineteenth century, for the Preface to the second edition of 1892 states that it was first published "long years ago when it appeared in the 'Western Guardian' ". This was a former Totnes newspaper. The novel is extremely romantic and absurdly inaccurate. It is based on the legend of a wicked sister who imprisons her sister Margaret so that she might inherit the castle. She and the Abbot of Torre, (referred to for some obscure reason as Ford Abbey), decide to poison the prisoner, but the Abbot, who administers the poison, does not give her a fatal dose, and keeps the poor woman for years in a secret vault beneath the castle. However, her lover—a de Clifford—rescues her, and she eventually regains her rights.

The intriguing point about the novel is that the writer insists that the castle chapel is in an undercroft beneath the building, and that there is a whole network of vaults and chambers adjoining it. It seems that anyone could visit the chapel at any time without going through the castle to get there. Is this all a complete myth, or could it be founded on facts—still half remembered when the book was written? In the Preface the writer states that the Pomeroys "estimated their power as little less than royal". The castle is referred to thus; "teeming as the spot does with tragic incident and legendary lore, throwing quite a mystic spell over the scene, it is but natural that a variety of tales should be associated therewith". This book is a valuable example of the way people of the mid nineteenth century surrounded the castle with an aura of myth and legend.

"A Secret of Berry Pomeroy" is a novel by Fred Wishaw with excellent illustrations by Frank Fellow. It was published in 1902, and so is the latest of the romantic novels about the castle. In this story the traditional legends and ghost stories are enacted by a gang of smugglers to mask their nefarious activities in the vicinity. Once again the presence of secret passages and underground caverns are insisted upon.

Elizabeth Barrett Browning's "Rhyme of the Duchess May" is considered in the chapter on Folklore. Her castle of Linteged may have been inspired by a visit to Berry Pomeroy. Certainly her knight on horseback leaping from the parapet of the castle rather than submit to a besieging army, smacks very much of the well known story of our castle.

"Berry Pomeroy Castle: A Historical and Descriptive Sketch" by T. C. and A. E. Mortimer, F.J.I., of the "Totnes Times" and "Western Guardian" was the official guide book to the castle for many a long year. I can remember it first in the 1920's and I am sure it was on sale for many years after that—possibly up to the 1940's when Edward Powley's "Illustrated Official Guide" superseded it. It was well written and reliable so far as the story of the castle was known at that time. An interesting paragraph in the Preface states:-"In compiling this sketch we have taken every care to procure trustworthy information, but in doing so we have experienced much difficulty, insomuch as the records of the castle, we are given to understand, are lost, having been lent by the 11th Duke of Somerset to a friend and never returned". Are these records still preserved in some remote country house, or else, perhaps, quietly mouldering to decay in a long-forgotten deedbox in a lawyer's office? One day, one hopes, they may reappear; and then perhaps all our preconceived notions about the castle will be in the melting-pot once more!

The booklet ran to 48 pages and had some excellent photographs in sepia tints, including the castle mill, church, Parliament Cottage, Compton Castle, etc. It was sold for 6d.—a sum which I found difficult to raise in my schooldays, and which my mother thought "quite expensive". It touched upon many subjects beside the castle—the geneaology of the Seymours, for instance, historical events, the folklore and ghosts. It still remains a very informative and readable booklet.

"Berry Pomeroy Castle" by Edward B. Powley, M.A., B.Litt., F.R.Hist.S. was the next official guide. It was brought out in 1947; on the back page of the cover it is explained that "This Guide is an abridged and adapted reprint, with selected but reduced sized photographs of the 'Introductory' and 'Castle' chapters contained in 'The House of de la Pomerai' by the same author, the photography for which was undertaken by 'Country Life' and the castle plan (H. M. Whitley) provided by courtesy of the Devonshire Association". It only contained two pages of photographs and Whitley's plan, with its, by then, admitted shortcomings in the northern corner. The reader is taken on a tour of the ruins, and may read about the doings of the Pomeroy and Seymour families, but there is no mention of anything else in the vicinity. By and large its appeal was perhaps not so obvious as the previous Guide by the brothers Mortimer, and it added very little to what had been said before.

"Annals of the Seymours" by H. St. Maur was published in 1902 by Kegan Paul, Trench, Trübner & Co. Ltd., London. It is a handsome book running to 534 pages, copiously adorned with no less than 70 illustrations, and containing 179 pages of Notes and Appendices. It is doubtful if many copies of this fine book were ever printed, for it would not have a wide appeal. The author gives detailed accounts of members of the family from its pre-Conquest origin in Normandy to the year 1884. Much out of the way information can be gathered from this book, the compiling of which must have taken many years. The author did for the Seymour family what Powley did for the Pomeroys. Many family portraits are reproduced; of particular interest is that of Lady Anne Seymour, at Knoyle, wife of the third Baronet. One cannot but wonder if this picture ever adorned the walls of Berry Pomeroy. Absorbing as the book may be, it really only concerns us in what it has to say of those generations of the family who actually lived at the castle. I am much indebted to the author for information concerning them which does not at present seem to be available from any other source.

The family were much to the fore in establishing William of Orange on the Throne; but at the same time the ex-King, James II, still carried on his Court in exile, as though his overthrow had never been. For instance on p.443 we find a letter from him inviting Sir Edward Seymour—the 4th Baronet—and a former member of the King's Privy Council, to come over to France with all haste so that he could be present at the birth of his next child which was then imminent. It was dated "at our castle of St. Germains, 2nd April, 1692, in the 8th year of our reign". How did the Baronet frame his reply?

The "Annals of the Seymours" is a rare book and makes good reading for all who have a bent for history.

CHAPTER 9

The Parish Church of St. Mary

At the time of the Domesday Survey Berry Pomeroy was a thriving and populous manor. It almost certainly had a church in Saxon times, therefore. How much of this was still standing in 1086 when the Survey was made we do not know. It was quite possibly rebuilt and enlarged in Norman times, the only remnant above ground being a part of a Norman capital of Purbeck marble found in the grounds of the old Vicarage in 1926. It now rests on the window sill of the westernmost window in the north aisle.

One of the earliest mentions of the church is in 1125 when Gosselin de la Pomerai gave it to his newly founded (or perhaps refounded) Abbey of St. Mary du Val in the diocese of Falaise, Normandy. This Abbey held the church until 1267 when, for convenience sake, it was exchanged for other ecclesiastical property with the Abbey of Merton in Surrey. It remained in the hands of the Priors of Merton until the dissolution, and it was they who appointed to the benefice.

Now the visitor will soon observe that there is no compact village at Berry Pomeroy, for the pattern is a church and manor house, farmhouses which are for the most part isolated, and a still more isolated castle. The mediaeval parish came right down to the River Dart, and included Bridgetown. This is, of course, no longer the case, but the resultant smaller parish is still entirely rural in character. The church stands at the bottom of the surrounding hills, yet it is so well placed that the lofty tower dominates the scene from whichever road one approaches. The building stands in a spacious churchyard which is set upon a bank high above the road on the south and west sides. With its ancient yew trees, variegated hollies and sunny position it is a pleasing sight at any time of year. The church is a dignified building in the late Perpendicular style. It has large windows, embattled aisles and turrets, and a fine south porch,

Church Tower from the North

all dominated by a tall tower of great strength and dignity. This tower has one or two unusual characteristics. In the first place it is not square; secondly, despite its height, it is only of two stages. Lastly it is devoid of pinnacles or any kind of ornamentation. Beneath its coat of stucco secrets may yet lurk. Professor Hoskins in "Devon" suggests that the whole thing is a 17th century rebuilding of an older tower. We shall see in a moment what the interior has to show us in support of such a theory.

The church is built of a mixture of limestone and red sandstone. These red and grey colours are assembled very skilfully and were not thrown together in a haphazard manner.

SOUTH PORCH

Sir Richard Pomeray (d.1496) is credited with the complete rebuilding of the church, and he saw to it that the south porch—the main entrance—was as impressive as possible. It was therefore endowed with an elaborately vaulted roof and a fine interior doorway. The vaulting is of two bays, with blank arcades to the east and west walls. It is supported upon six elegant shafts. There are Tudor roses on the third and fifth bosses in the ceiling and these give a clue to the identity of the crowned head on the same rib, and also to the female head. The marriage of King Henry VII with Elizabeth of York was a strategic step which united the rival factions of York and Lancaster, thus putting an end to the hateful Wars of the Roses. Henry ascended the throne in 1485, and at that period carved heads of the couple were frequently chosen by masons to decorate their buildings, just as we see them here. So if the heads here are those of King Henry VII and his Queen, it is safe to date the rebuilding of this stately church as not long after 1485. All this accords with the style of the building. The outer doorway to the porch is square-headed, with heavy hood moulding. There are quatrefoil spandrels. The inner doorway is less heavy in style and of considerable beauty. Did its doors once fill the central doorway of the screen? There is a stoup on the east side and also another just inside the door. The parvise above has a small window of two lights. It is reached by a stair turret at the SW corner of the aisle which continues to the roof. A vestry in the SE angle of the south aisle and a stoke-hole are well constructed modern additions, embattled like the aisles. A slate sundial over the porch door dates from 1686.

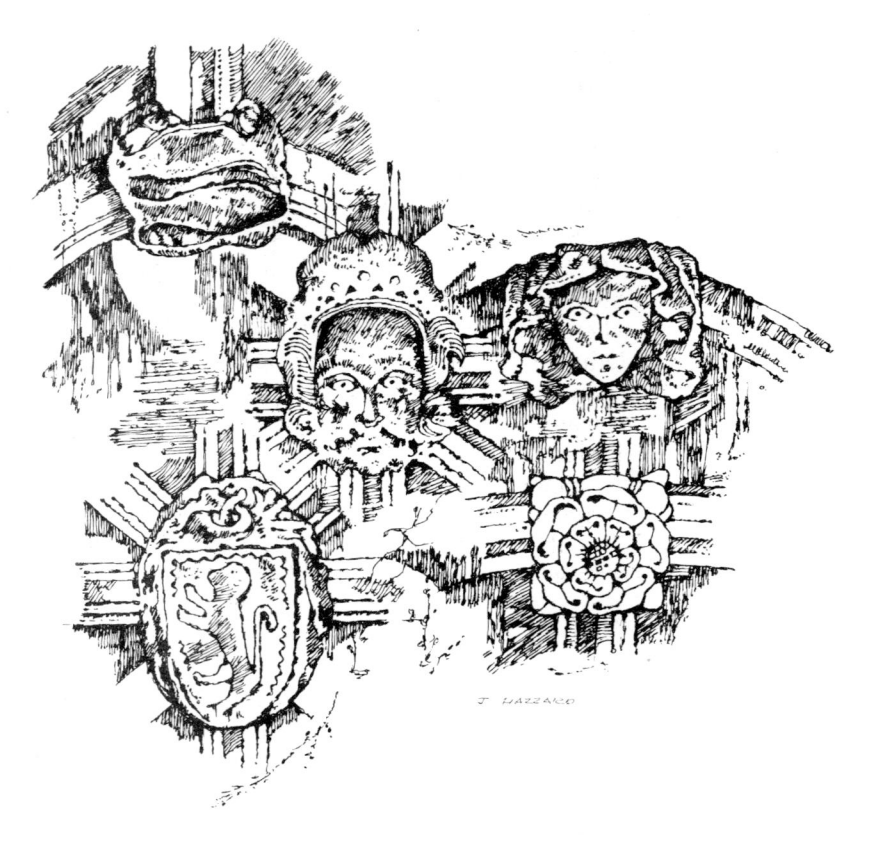

Berry Pomeroy Church-roof bosses in porch

NAVE

The entry to the church from the porch has no step, and, when the doors stand open, this fact adds much to the spaciousness of the approach. Indeed spaciousness is the chief characteristic of this church, particularly the Nave whose arcade continues in an unbroken line beyond the screen into the Chancel. Such a characteristic is common, however, in Devon churches of this period; a continuous roofline, unbroken from end to end of the building, is always impressive. In the case of St. Mary's the Nave is unusually wide—24ft.6in. as against a mere 10ft.6in. in the aisles. The roof is therefore spread at a wide angle. An exterior view shows that it covers the aisles as well, but this is not apparent from within. Now the reason for the wide Nave is a fascinating one. The Normans in their building frequently used the measure of a sagene (7ft.). The church, with the exception of the chancel and chapels, measures up in sagenes. From this one can deduce that the present church was built on the foundations of the Norman church which still support the nave arcade. The length from tower step to Chancel step is 49ft. (7 sagenes), the width is 24ft.6in. (3½ sagenes); width from pillar to pillar is 10ft.3in. (1¾ sagenes). But the Chancel, whose length is 26ft.4in., cannot be divided into the old measure, so it was evidently completely new when the church was rebuilt in the 15th century.

What can we deduce from all these statistics? (1) That the total length of the Norman church was 49ft.; (2) Its total width whether it had an aisle or not was the same as the present Nave; (3) The arcade could rest on the bases of the former Norman walls; (4) Since the aisle width is 1½ sagenes this suggests that there were small transepts of this length, the church in that case being cruciform; (5) The tower step probably rests on a Norman foundation, and the higher level of its floor may be the level of the floor of the Norman church.

TOWER

The tower is separated from the nave by a lofty arch. It is to be noticed that the wide west doorway has a pointed arch, and so has the staircase doorway. All this points to the fact that the tower is older, possibly by a century or more, than the rest of the perpendicular church. It much resembles the neighbouring tower at Ipplepen which is earlier than the church. Both towers taper and are of greater strength than the more slender 15th century towers. The very fact that it is not square is reminiscent of the towers at Coffinswell and East Ogwell which are early towers and have this characteristic. There is really no internal evidence that the tower was ever rebuilt. The dominant feature of the interior is the large recess on the south side. It has a low, undressed arch about 12 feet in height. The depth of the recess is 3ft.3in., and there are shelves of Beer stone at each end; that at the east end being higher than its companion at the west end. It could have been a tomb or even a narrow chantry chapel—possibly a combination of both. There is no certainty about either suggestion, however.

The fact that the tower is not square is more easy to understand when one sees the considerable width of the Nave. The exterior measurements are 28ft (N to S) and 24ft. (E to W). To have put an extra four feet on the east to west measurement would have greatly added to the cost of building. So the old builders risked making the sides uneven, because they knew very well that the defect would never be noticed unless pointed out.

ARCADE

The Nave is divided from the aisles by a graceful arcade of Beer stone. The peculiarity of the south arcade is that the capitals are adorned with the names of benefactors who possibly provided the money to build it. The inscriptions form E to W (1) are:- Johes Letin, Alys ux ei; (2) Johes Oldreeve—then the screen covers a damaged inscription; (3) Johes Godrigge, Witha ux ei; (4) Edwards Lane, Jona ux ei; (5) Ricard Condor, Alys ux ei; (6) Et pro omnibus benefactoribus huius operi orate.

SCREEN

The splendid oak screen which separates Nave and Chancel is 46ft. in length. It has three doorways. Pevsner describes it as "one of the most perfect in Devon, not only complete in that it extends from north to south wall, but also in having its original coving, its cornice (with only one band of decoration), and its cresting". The painted figures on the wainscoting are cut short at the knees. Arthur Ellis, in his pamphlet "Some Ancient Churches Around Torquay", has listed the 24 figures and attempted to identify them, in spite of the fact that several are much mutilated. A rood stairway on the north side continues upward to give access to the roof by way of an embattled turret.

CHANCEL

It is separated from what were once north and south chapels by parclose screens. Here the old colours have been obscured by brown paint and graining. The treasure of the chancel is the ornate altar tomb of Sir Richard Pomeray and his wife, formerly Elizabeth Densell. Prince describes it as "fine, fretted and flowered". It has already been fully accounted for.

ORGAN

The former South Chapel is occupied by the organ. It is a very superior instrument of pleasing tone. Unfortunately the builder is not known, but quite possibly it was J. W. Walker of London, several of whose instruments are in the locality. Its date would be c.1875/85. The specification is as follows:

Great Organ		Swell Organ		Pedal Organ	
Open Diapason	8'	Open Diapason	8'	Bourdon	16'
Gamba	8'	Stopped Diapason		**Couplers**	
Stopped Diapason	8'	treble	8'	Swell to Great	
Principal	4'	Stopped Diapason		Swell to Pedal	
Flute	4'	bass	8'	Great to Pedal	
Fifteenth	2'	Principal	4'		
Mixture	2rks	Piccolo	2'		
		Oboe	8'		

NORTH CHAPEL

What would be the north chapel in mediaeval days became in post-Reformation days the Seymours' family "pew". The doorway by which the family would enter is just south of the huge monument. Here, presided over by the effigies of their forbears, they worshipped each Sunday. The tomb is thus described by Dugdale:- "Berry Pomeroy church which was built by one of the Pomeroy family contains a splendid alabaster monument to the memory of Lord Edward Seymour, knight, son of the Duke of Somerset; Edward Seymour, Baronet and his Lady, the daughter of Sir Arthur Champernoune. The two first are represented in armour; the knight having a truncheon in his hand and lying cross-legged. The lady is in a black dress, with the figure of a child in a cradle, at her head, and at her feet another in a chair: below are nine kneeling figures with books open before them. This monument was repaired by the late Duke of Somerset, the eighth lineal descendant of the Duke of Somerset the Protector." (From Dugdale's "The New British Traveller" (Devonshire), 1819.)

The once splendid colours are today faded, and it is to be hoped that in the not too distant future they may be restored, so that the whole of this corner of the church may be ablaze with colour as once it used to be. Pevsner says unkind things about this tomb; "The figures astonishingly naive" he says; "to think that the children and grandchildren of Lord Protector Somerset were satisfied with this!" Nevertheless most people will not agree with his verdict, for the figures, though quaintly placed, are not unusual for the period and are of a restrained dignity. The whole monument compares favourably with others of that age to be seen in Exeter Cathedral or Westminster Abbey.

WINDOWS

The windows are large—particularly those of the aisles; they do not appear to have their original tracery, however. Early examples of the work of C. W. Whall fills the east window and its supporters in the north and south walls. The glass dates from c.1889. The East Window shows "Christ the object of our worship and hope". He is depicted holding a globe celestial on which are seven stars which represent the seven churches. The north window shows the Adoration of the Magi, whilst that on the south side shows Christ in the Temple, with the doctors of the law.

Westcote's account of the stained glass "armouries" has already been given on p.135. This was written in the 17th century, and today only six coats of arms which he describes have survived. There are two at the top of the east window in the north chapel, three in the corresponding window on the south side, and one at the west end of the south aisle. In Westcote's day there were shields of 17 different families—Pomeroy occurring four times. They seem for the most part to have belonged to the families which married into the Pomeroy family. The coats of arms of England and France were also displayed. Arthur Mee states that this is 15th century glass. If he is right, then perhaps Sir Richard had arranged in the windows a display of family heraldry.

FONT

The old Norman font has not survived, and the present octagonal font dates from the period of the rebuilding. It is of pleasing proportions and contains its original lead lining and staples.

ALTAR RAILS

At the west end of the north aisle a former altar and communion rails are still preserved. They are of 17th century date and follow the Laudian arrangement whereby the altar was enclosed on three sides by communion rails.

LIST OF VICARS

At the west end of the Nave stands a list of vicars from 1259 onwards which are carved on handsome oak panels. This gift was made by Susan, wife of Algernon, 15th Duke of Somerset in 1918.

The list is as follows:-

1259 Richard de Motbiry
1328 Sir Roger Oseway
1340 Sir Robert de la Reye
     Sir Stephen Atte Fosshe
1361 Sir Reginald de Horsyngtone (see p.p.35, 57)
1391 Sir John Stakeforde
1399 Sir Walter Dommewylle
1414 Sir William Clouburghe (d.Sept.)
1442 Sir John Wylyam
     Sir Thomas Lake
1469 Master John Wyghte
1487 Master William Hillyage
1503 Master John Southewode
1506 Mst. Edmund Wylfforde
1507 Sir George Faryngdone
1542 Peter Maynwarynge
1549 John Rixmane
1567 Ambrose Tonye
1575 Thomas Wrighte

1586 Edward Procter
1636 William Randall
1681 John Prince
1723 Joseph Fox
1781 John Edwards
1834 Edward Brown
1843 William Burrough Cosens
1862 Arthur Joseph Everett
1896 Henry Stewart Prinsep
1908 Herbert Cooper
1915 William Aitchison
1921 Herbert Eustace, Preb. of Exeter Cathedral
1927 William Outram
1935 Herbert Mackworth Drake, Preb. of Exeter Cathedral
1944 Edward Joseph Gawne
1954 Edward Shewell
1978 Ronald Harry Baker

SEYMOUR MEMORIALS

Besides the large monument already mentioned there are:-

(1) A heart-shaped brass on the east wall of the north chapel which reads "Alexander Seymour/Esqr/Son of the Honble Sir Edward/Seymour of Maiden Bradley in the County of Wilts Bartt/departed this life April 3rd 1731/aged 30".

(2) The window above is to the memory of Algernon, 15th Duke of Somerset and Susan Margaret, his wife. He died October 22nd, 1923. He carried the orb at the coronations of Edward VII and George V. The window is by the daughter of C. W. Whall, Miss Veronica Whall.

Approach to Church Porch

(3) In the churchyard Archibald Algernon Henry Seymour, 13th Duke of Somerset, is commemorated by a large granite tombstone. He died January 16th, 1891.

MEMORIALS TO VICARS

Perhaps the most worthy of note is the memorial to the Rev. John Prince, author of the "Worthies of Devon". A copy is in possession of the church. This was published in folio in 1702 and there was a second edition in quarto in 1810. The memorial is a tablet on the north wall of the chancel. It reads:-

"In memory of the Revd. John Prince, A.M., vicar of this parish and author of the Worthies of Devon. He was instituted in the year 1681 and died on the 9th day of Sepr., 1723. Also of the Revd. Joseph Fox, A.M., successor of the above. He died on the 1st day of Feby., 1781 aged 88".

There is a memorial to the Revd. John Edwards, 1781-1834 and also to the Revd. Henry Stewart Prinsep which takes the form of a stained glass window on the south side of the Chancel. This has already been described.

RESTORATION OF CHURCH

This was carried out in 1878/9 at a cost of over £3,000. An entirely new roof superseded the old one which was "curiously painted with clouds and gilt stars to represent the firmament". The names of the churchwardens Richard Tully and Edward Shinner, 1698, were also inscribed beneath. So it looks as though the church lost its original roof in 1698; what we see today is the third roof. An old photo taken before the restoration shows behind the altar the Lord's Prayer, Creed and Commandments. There were "horsebox" pews and a three decker pulpit. All of these were swept away, and no doubt the "snail" pointing on the lovely red sandstone walls dates from this time.

REGISTERS

They date from 1602, but there are no churchwardens accounts before 1801.

CLOCK

This dates from 1772. A minute from a vestry meeting of that year states "unanimously concluded and agreed to have a parish clock in the tower". Mr. John Windeatt (of Totnes?) was ordered to contract for a good and substantial clock to be fixed aforesaid, in the best manner he shall think fit". This clock had no face, but in 1887, to commemorate Queen Victoria's Jubilee, a face was added.

BELLS

I am grateful to the Rev. J. G. M. Scott, adviser on bells and belfries to the Guild of Devonshire Ringers, for the following notes on the bells.

The first information which we have of any bells at Berry Pomeroy is in a report of the Commissioners of Church goods in 1552. They stated that there were "iiij belles yn the towr their". With recastings at various times the ring remained a four until 1897.

The oldest bell in the present ring is the tenor, cast in 1607 by John Byrdall of Exeter, the last of the men who worked the old Exeter bell foundry, which lasted from 1380 until John's death in 1624. This is an excellent bell of good tone, and one of the best surviving bells by this founder.

Next comes the 5th, cast in 1635 by Thomas Pennington of Exeter, then the 7th by Ambrose Gooding of Plymouth, who worked during the first half of the 18th century. After the date this bell has a profile head of a king, probably George I or II.

The 6th was recast in 1829 by Thomas Mears of London; there is no record of the earlier bell.

In 1897 the ring was increased to a six, the two new bells being cast by John Warner of Cripplegate.

In 1919 two further bells were added by the Whitechapel foundry. This addition had been awaited for ten years, for when Harry Stokes built the frame in 1909 he provided eight pits. The frame is of cast iron, and the bells are hung in plain bearings with the exception of the 7th which at some time has been hung in ball bearings.

The three oldest bells bear the name of the Goodridge family, one of whose names has already been mentioned among those names carved on the capitals of the 15th century Nave arcade.

The weight of the tenor is about 17 cwt.

Inscriptions:-
Treble 28¾ diameter, note E. Mears and Stainbank Founders, London. "In honorem Dei et in piam memoriam Henrici Stewart Prinsep hujus ecclesiae per annos XII vicarii A.D.MCMIX.

Laudate Dominum In Sanctis Eius."
2nd. 29½ diameter, note D sharp. As above except for bottom line which reads:- "Sit Nomen Domini Benedictum".
3rd. 30¾ diameter, note C sharp. Cast by John Warner and Sons Ltd., London, 1897. "To the Glory of God and in Memory of Admiral G. H. May and Letitia, his Wife."
4th. 32¼ diameter, note B. Cast by John Warner and Sons Ltd., London, 1897. "In Memory of Dynson Wilmot Hennett, 1897."
5th. 33¼ diameter, note A. "Richard Govdridge Robart Dinnyng Church Wardens T   P:1635."
6th. 7⅜ diameter, note G sharp. T. Mears of London, fecit 1829. "God protect our Church and King. Mr. John Searle, Mr. Richard Quint, Churchwardens."
7th. 40¼ diameter, note F sharp. "Ino. Lyde. Roger. Goodridge. Gent^l. Ward^s. A   Gooding. 1751." (King's head after date).
Tenor 44¾ diameter, note E. "Ambrose * Goodridge * Nycolas * Dart * Wardens   Anno Do   1607   ."

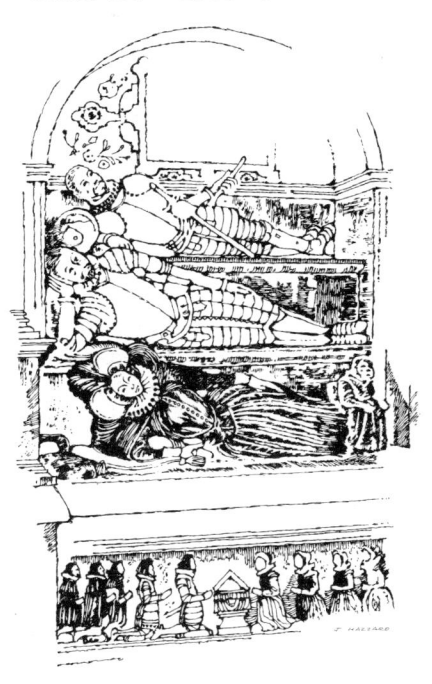

The Seymour Tomb

First Floor Entrance to Great Parlour

CHAPTER 10

Botany

by Ellaline Jerrard

Berry Pomeroy has many charms. Its old world atmosphere of serenity and "something"—not of this material world—is strongly to be felt.

One can almost step into another dimension of time. I find myself completely embraced by it whenever I visit the Castle.

In late summer the vivid blue of Alkenet was mixed with the mauve-pink of that beautiful wild Geranium "Herb Robert"; and near a wall was a new and bright Ivy Broomrape looking like an imitation Orchid. Growing out of an upper window of St. Margaret's Tower was a flourishing Dog Rose which must have established itself long years ago.

For all who are interested in wild flowers, the following list, compiled in late summer, will serve as a mere sample. In Spring and early Summer there will be many others, according to their season of blooming.

Bellis perennis	Common Daisy
Sonchus olearacius	Sow Thistle
Hieracium umbellatus	Leafy Hawkweed
Crepis capillaris	Smooth Hawksbeard
Senicio jacobaea	Common Ragwort

Circium vulgare	Spear Thistle
Achillea millefolium	Yarrow
Arctium minus	Lesser Burdock
Eupatorium cannabinum	Hemp Agrimony
Geranium robertianum	Herb Robert
Geranium purpureum	Lesser Herb Robert (Little Robin)
Geranium molle	Dovesfoot Cranesbill
Cymbalaria muralis	Ivy leaved Toadflax
Digitalis purpurea	Foxglove
Pentaglottis sempervirens	Alkenet
Parietaria diffusa	Pellitory-of-the-Wall
Pastinaca sativa	Wild Parsnip
Sanicula europaea	Sanicle
Umbilicus rupestris	Pennywort
Galium mollugo	Hedge Bedstraw
Plantago lanceolata	Ribwort Plaintain
Plantago major	Great Plaintain
Myosotis arvensis	Common Forget-me-not
Trifolium campestre	Hop Trefoil
Vicia hirsuta	Hairy Tare
Medicago lupulina	Black Medick or "Nonsuch"
Orobanche hederae	Ivy Broomrape
Rosa canina	Dog Rose
Rubus caesius	Dewberry
Rubus fruticosus	Blackberry
Geum urbanum	Herb Bennet
Ranunculus acris	Meadow Buttercup
Silene dioica	Red Campion
Cerastium glomeratum	Clustered Mouse-ear

Circaea lutetiana	Enchanters Nightshade
Chamaenerion angustifolium	Rosebay Willowherb
Epilobium lanceolatum	Spear-leaved Willowherb
Primula vulgaris	Primrose
Viola riviniana	Common Violet
Hypericum perforatum	Common St. John's Wort
Iris foetidissima	Gladdon
Euphorbia helioscopia	Sun Spurge
Prunella vulgaris	Self-heal
Malva sylvestris	Common Mallow
Stachys sylvatica	Hedge Woundwort

Recorded during May 1982

Endymion non-scriptus	Bluebell
Veronica chamaedrys	Germander Speedwell
Allium ursinum	Ramsons
Galeobdolon luteum	Archangel
Geranium lucidum	Shining Cranesbill
Alliaria petiolata	Garlic Mustard
Galium aparine	Cleavers
Glechoma hederacea	Ground Ivy
Stellaria holostea	Greater Stitchwort
Euphorbia amygdaloides	Wood Spurge
Crataegus monogyna	Common Hawthorn
Smyrnium olusatrum	Alexanders
Torilis japonica	Hedge Parsley

Rampart Stairs

INDEX 1
Persons & Places

A
Alric 43, 44
Afton 1, 25, 68
Anne, Queen 84

B
Barrett Browning, Elizabeth 96
Bathonia, Iseult (w. of Henry
 (VI) de la Pomerai) 52
Battlebury 92
BERRY POMEROY,
 Barton of 124
 Castle
  Chapel (possible) 32
  Colonnade 37
  Courtyard 37
  Curtain Wall 20
  Fresco 9, 31, 61
  Gatehouse 29-32
  Kitchens 39
  Lodge 13,121
  Pomeroys' manorhouse 16, 19, 53
  Rampart Walk 32
  St. Margaret's Tower 13, 20, 32-35
 Capital messuage of 28
 Church of St. Mary 59, 145-157
 Advowson of Church of St. Mary 68
 Deer parks at 9, 16, 60, 121-125
 Deer park, mansion in 124
 Manor of Beri, Byri,
  Byry, Bury) 15, 43, 44, 45, 46, 129
 Manor house of, 15, 16, 28, 53
Beville, Margaret (w. of Edward
 Pomeray of Tregony) 59
Bradworthy, church of 49
 manor of 49
Brantyngham, Thomas de,
 Bishop of Exeter 55, 56
Bray, Mrs. 14, 99, 106, 137
Brewer, Lord William 49
Bridgetown (Brigg, Bridgetown
 Pomeroy) 51, 54, 62, 145
Brixham, manor of 19, 55, 57, 58, 62
Bronescombe, Walter,
 Bishop of Exeter 51
Broom Park Barn 121, 125
Buckfast Abbey 45
 Abbot of
 refounding of 45

C
Carminou, Elizabeth 55
 (w. of Henry (VIII) de la Pomerai)
Carnell, Anne (2nd w. of Henry 173
 Pomeray (X))
Cary, George (of Cockington) 69, 70
Caunville, Amicia (w. of Henry (VII)
 de la Pomerai) 53, 55
Champernowne, Elizabeth (w. of Sir
 Edward Seymour (III)) 69
Chanctonbury Ring, Sussex 88
Charles I, King 73
Charles II, King 75
Cole, John 56, 57, 58
Combes, Luke M. 136
Compton Castle 19, 23
Copplestone, Sir John 75
Corbet, Piers 52
Cornwall, Reginald, Earl of 47
Crecy, Battle of 55
Cumings, Mrs. 100, 136

D
Dartmouth 69, 70, 72, 130
 castle of 75
Densell. Elizabeth (w. of Sir Richard
 Pomeray) 59, 60, 61
Desborough, General 75
Devon, Sheriffs of 52, 56, 58, 59, 69, 70
 Lieutenants of 69
Drake, Sir Francis 69

E
Edgcumbe, Joan (w. of Sir Thomas
 Pomerey (II))) 62
Edward VI, King 67, 68
Elizabeth I, Queen 68, 70
Emma (w. of Gosselin de la
 Pomerai) 46
Excavations 9, 37
Exeter, Castle of 52
 Cathedral of 46, 52
 Dominican Friars at 52, 60

F
Falaise (Normandy) 15, 43, 46
 diocese of
Farquhar, Sir Walter 25, 109, 116-118

163

Fillol, Catherine (1st w. of Lord
   Protector)   see Pedigree
Fleet Mill Creek   74

G
Ganne, Chateau (Normandy)   15, 43, 48
Gatcombe Brook   11, 121
Gilberte, Sir John   69
Gloucester, Abbey of St. Peter   45
Goodridge (Goodrich, Godrigge,
   Govdridge), John   150

H
Harberton (Hurberton),
   manor of   19, 55, 57, 62
Henry I, King   46, 47
   " II
   " III   47
   " IV   57
   " VII   59, 61
   " VIII   61, 65, 68
Hempston, Little   124
Hidesburga (Bradworthy)   49
Historians:-
   Dugdale   136
   Hooker   133
   Leland   133
   Lysons   136
   Maton   135
   Pole   135
   Polwhele   136
   Prince   see under that name
   Risdon   133, 134
   Westcote   133, 134
Horsyngton, Reginald de
   (vicar of Berry Pomeroy)   55, 57

J
James I, King   70, 72
   II "   76, 143, 144
John, Prince (later King John)   50

K
Killegrew, Dorothy   72
   (w. of Sir Edward Seymour (IV))

M
Maiden Bradley, Wilts   67, 75, 77, 83
Margaret,   35, 97
   St. Margaret's Tower
   (see Berry Pomeroy Castle)
Marston Moor, battle of   75
Mary, Queen   68

Maurice, Prince;
   letters of   130
Merton, Joan (w. of Sir John
   de la Pomerai)   56
Merton Priory, Surrey   46, 52, 145
Mill, Castle   13, 129
Montague, Edward   41
Musselburgh, Battle of   67
Moles, Joan de   55

N
Negelle, the castle cook   40
Netherton (Nitheway),
   in Brixham   56, 57, 58
Netherton (Berry Pomeroy)   123

O
Orange, William of   76, 77, 84
   (King William III)

P
Paignton, bishop's park at   51
Park, see Berry Pomeroy,
   deerparks at,
Park Corner   121
Parliament,
   Members of   56, 57, 71, 72, 84
Parr, Queen Katherine (relict of
   King Henry VIII)   see Pedigree
Plymouth, siege of   75
Pollard, Sir Hugh   69
POMEROY (de la Pomerai, Pomeraio,
   Poumerai, Pomeray, Pomerey,
   Pumerey)
   De la Pomerai:-
      Beatrix   44
      Ethelward   45
      Gosselin   15, 46, 145
      Henry (I)   47
      Henry (II)   19, 48, 49, 127, 139
      Henry (III)   49, 50
      Henry (IV)   50
      Henry (V)   51
      Henry (VI)   51, 52
      Henry (VII)   19, 53
      Henry (VIII)   55
      Henry (IX)   55
      Joan   55
      Joanna   57
      John   55, 129
      Ralf   15, 43-45
      Thomas I Sir   54, 56, 57

Valentine	56
William	45
William Capra	44
Pomeray:-	
Edward I of Tregony	21, 27, 55, 56, 57, 58
Elizabeth Lady	27, 39
Henry (X)	59
Seintclere, Sir	59
Richard, Sir	59, 147
Pomerey:-	
Edward II, Sir	61
John, Sir	20, 21, 28
Thomas II, Sir	62, 63, 67
Pomeroy:-	
Eleanor, Lady	35
Margaret, Lady	35
Pomeroy's Leap	24, 93
Pommerai, La, Normandy	43
Popham, Laetitia (2nd w. of Sir Edward Seymour (VI))	see Pedigree
Popham, Laetitia (w. of Sir Edward (Seymour (VII))	see Pedigree
Portman, Anne (w. of Sir Edward Seymour (V))	74, 76, 78-82
Potter, Barnaby, bishop of Carlisle	71
Powley, Edward B.	43, 51, 54, 93, 128, 140, 141
Prince, Rev. John	9, 35, 38, 40, 44, 60, 106

R

Ralegh, Alice (w. of Henry Pomeray (X))	59
Richard, I, King	19, 48, 127
Ridgeway, Sir John	70
Rohesia (nat. d. of King Henry I)	47
Rohesia (d. of Thomas Bardolf the elder)	48

S

St. Marychurch, William de	128
St. Michael's Mount	48, 49, 95, 136
Sandridge	55, 62, 63
Sapcotes, Joan (w. of Sir Edward Pomerey (II))	61, 62
Sapcotes, Sir John	28
Scanes, John	43, 44, 45
Seymour, Sir Edward (I) Duke of Somerset and Lord Protector	65-67

Sir Edward (II), "Lord" Seymour	67-69
Sir Edward (III), Bart.	69-71
Sir Edward (IV), Bart.	72-74, 122
Sir Edward (V), Bart	74-82
Sir Edward (VI), Bart., Speaker of House of Commons	83, 84, 144
Sir Edward (VII), Bart.	see Pedigree
Sir Edward (VIII) Bart., succeeded as 8th Duke of Somerset	84
Queen Jane (w. of King Henry VIII)	65-66
Sir John (of Wolfhall)	65
Sir John (son of Lord Protector)	67
Sir Thomas, cr. Lord Sudeley	see Pedigree
Shadrack	125
Stanhope, Anne, second w. of Lord Protector	see Pedigree
Stockleigh Pomeroy	57, 58, 62
Summer Hill	125
Swete, Rev. J. B.	13

T

Tavistock Abbey, Abbot of	60
Torre Abbey	16, 49, 69, 99
Abbot of	60
Totnes	75
castle of	75
Tregony, Manor of	15, 19, 53, 54, 55, 57, 58, 59
Mayor and Corporation of	61
Treseder, R.	42

V

Val du, Abbey of Notre Dame (Normandy)	15, 46, 48, 49, 52, 145
Viteri, Matilda de	48

W

Wale, Margaret (w. of Sir Edward Seymour (VI))	see Pedigree
Walsh, Jane (w. of Sir Edward Seymour (II),	68
Weekaborough	91, 92
Wicganbeorg, battle of	91, 92
Wishaw, Fred	105, 142
Wishing Tree	87
Wood, Mrs. Henry	140

INDEX 2
Subjects

A
"Annals of the Seymours"   71, 116, 130, 143, 175

B
Baronage   55
Baronetcy   70
BERRY POMEROY CASTLE:-
Books about:- (i) Guide Book by T. C. & A. E. Mortimer   142
(ii) Guide Book by E. B. Powley   143
Novels:- (i) The Castle of Berry Pomeroy" by Edward Montague   141
(ii) "Henry de Pomeroy" by Mrs. Bray   137
(iii) "A Secret of Berry Pomeroy" by Fred Wishaw   142
(iv) "Pomeroy Abbey" by Mrs. Henry Wood   140
Poems:- (i) "Berry Pomeroy" by Luke M. Combes   130
(ii) part of poem by Mrs. Cuming.
building of   19-21, 37-42
dating of   8, 17-20, 42
demolition of   83
fire (theory of destruction by)   105
fortification of   20, 28
Norman castle (theory of)   15, 44
Black Death   19, 28
Botany   9, 159-161

C
Cannonballs   104, 105
Chesne, du, "Historiae Normannorum"   43
Civil War   73-76, 91
Commons, House of   84
Conquest, Norman   43
Crown, debt to   19, 57
Crusades   50

D
Dartmouth, Castle,
Governorship of   74
siege of castle   74
Devon, John Donn's map of   123
Inside front cover
Documentation:-
Pomeroy era (at Wiltshire County Record Office, Trowbridge, and at P.R.O. Chancery Lane, London)   127
Seymour era (at Wiltshire County Record Office, Trowbridge, and at Devon County Record Office, Exeter)   129
confirmation of lands to Henry (II) de la Pomerai from King Richard I   127
Dry Stone Walling Association   122

E
Environment, Ministry of   8, 15, 41
Exeter, siege of   44, 45

F
Familia, royal (king's "privata familia")   51
Field names, old   125
Folklore:-
bombardment of castle   104
fire, destruction by   105
invincibility of castle   88-90
imprisonment of Lady Margaret   97
Kidnapped heiress   99
Passages, underground   103
Pomeroys in folklore   92, 93
Pomeroy's Leap   93
"Rhyme of Duchess May"   96, 97
Silver Spurs   98
Treasure, hidden   100
Siege of castle   91
Unfortunate lovers   98
Unwanted infant   100
Wishing Tree   87

G
Galleons, captured Spanish   69
Ghosts:-
recent experiences (i) at Castle;   110-116
(ii) Gatcombe Valley;   110, 111, 112-115
traditional ghosts
(i) The lady in blue dress   116-119
(ii) The lady in white dress   116-119
(iii) Unfortunate lovers   116-119
Gold, Field of Cloth of   61
Grant (to Sir John Sapcotes)   128

H
Heraldry   55, 56, 172, 175

I

Indulgence (from Pope Clement VIII)	55
Invasions, Threat of French	20, 56
Threat of Spanish	69
Inventory (1688)	77

K

Knights' fees	51, 54, 55
Knighthood	55, 56, 57, 58, 61, 63

L

Lefournier, "Essaye Historique sur l'Abbaye de Notre Dame du Val"	48
Letters:-	
from Lord Bath	129
from King Charles I	130
from Prince Maurice	130
from Sir Edward Seymour (III)	78-82

M

Mass, licence for celebration of	56
Modbury, Muster at	73

O

Orange, landing of Prince William of	76
Oxford, Provisions of	52

P

Pardon from King Richard I	128

Pedigrees:-	
Pomeroy	172-3
Seymour	175

R

Restoration of Monarchy	73, 76

S

Sagene	149
Seymour, Sir Edward (V), letters of	78-82
Somerset:-	
Dukedom of	66, 67
Papers	26, 57, 77, 122
Supernatural (see Ghosts)	
Surveys:-	
Domesday	43, 44
1292	15, 53, 122, 128

T

Tithes, "overlooked"	60
Transactions of Devonshire Association (T.D.A.)	43, 54, 122, 128

V

Valletort Estates	50, 52, 54, 55
lawsuits concerning	

W

Wars (Welsh)	52
Western Rising	62
Wildflowers	159-161
Wishing Tree	87

Old print of Berry Pomeroy Castle from the north

Top of Stairwell

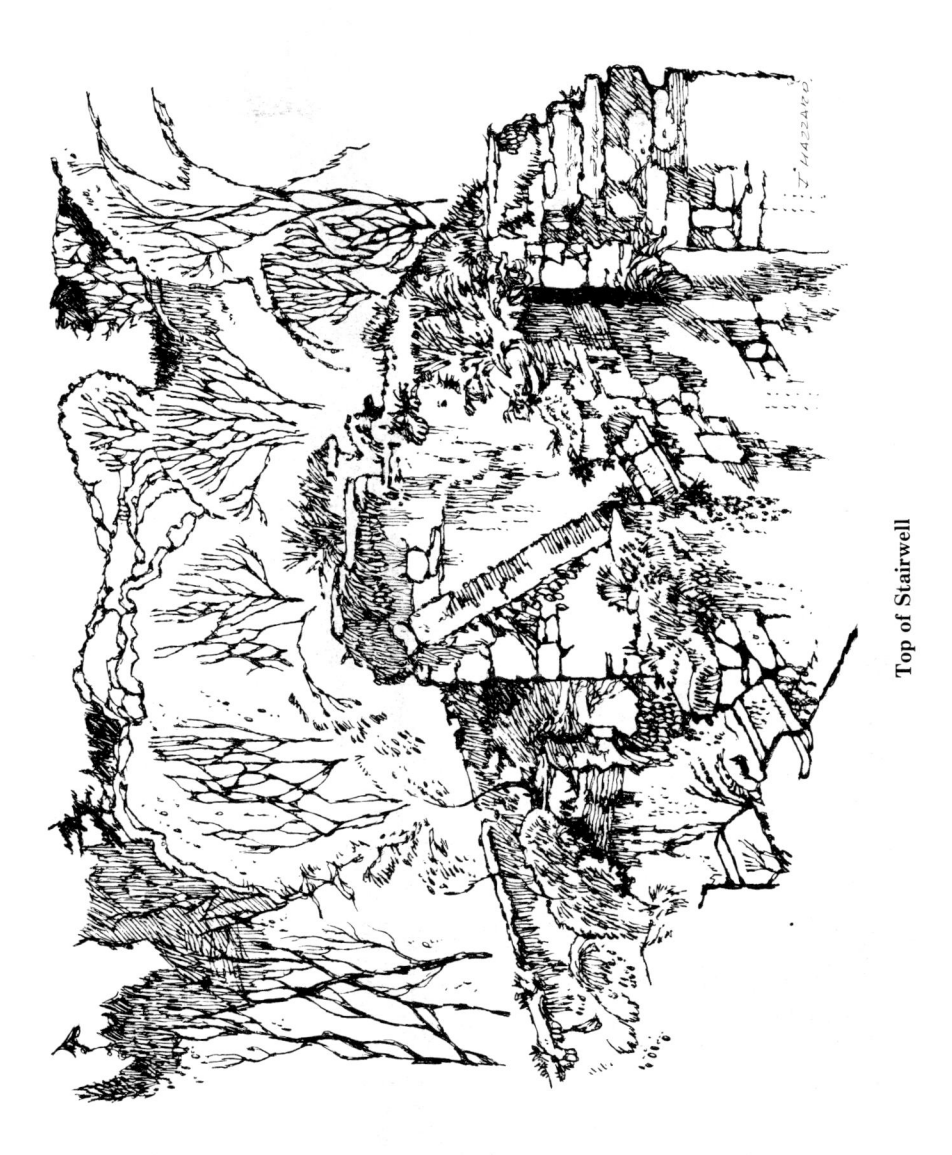

Remaining stacks in Seymour wing

Cellar in Seymour Wing (now filled in).

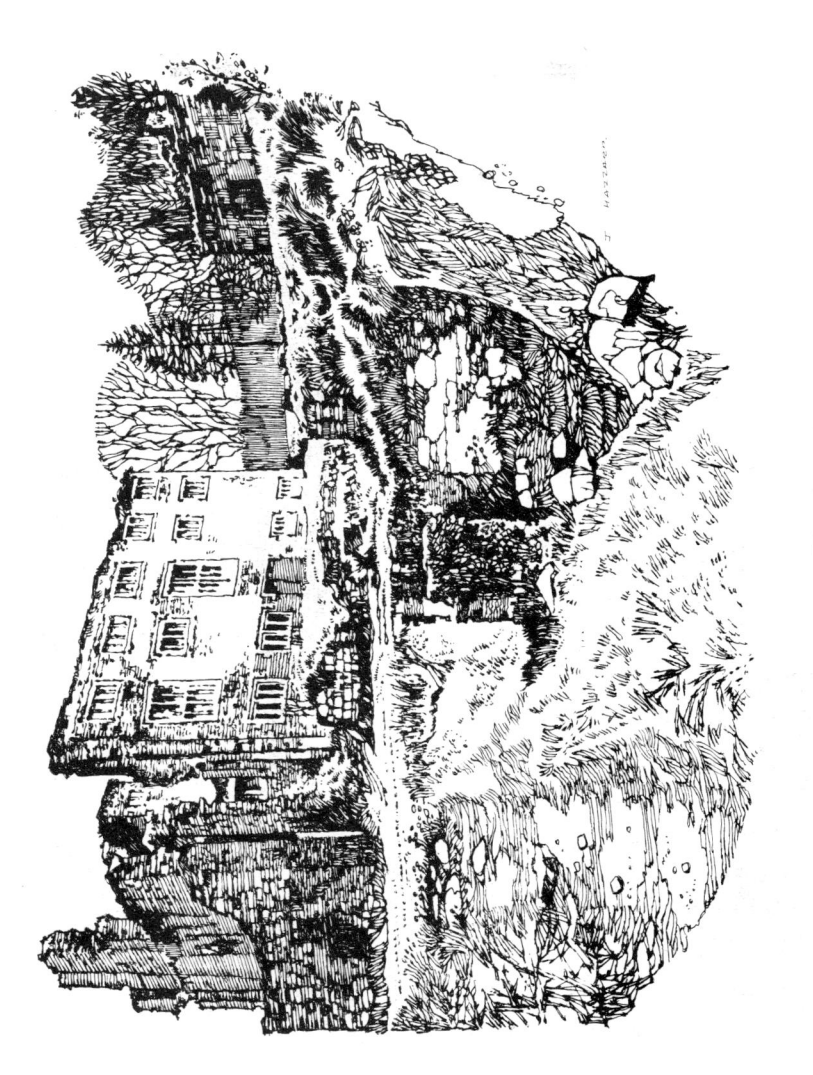

THE POMEROYS OF BERRY

FIGURES DENOTE SUCCESSIVE OWNERS OF THE MANOR

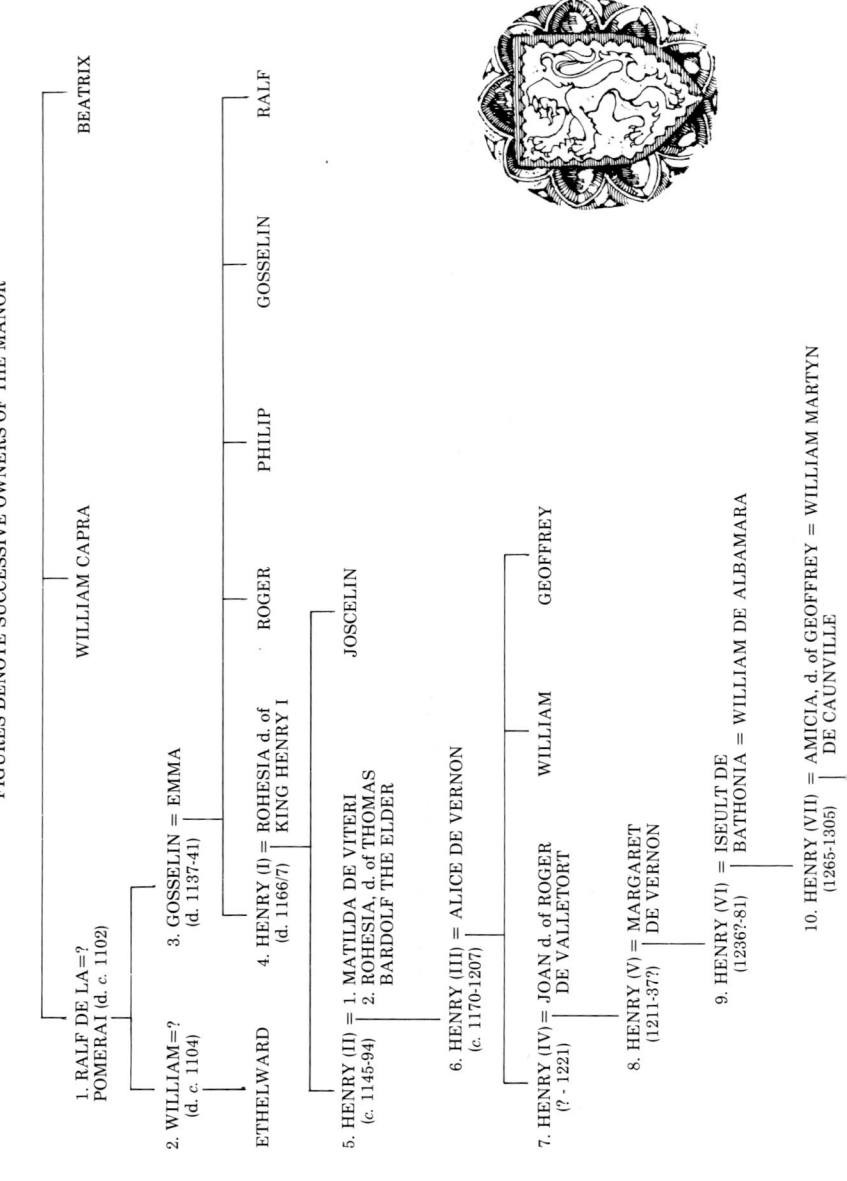

```
                                          WILLIAM CAPRA ─────────────── BEATRIX
                                               │
   ┌───────────────────────────────────────────┼──────────────────────────────────┐
1. RALF DE LA = ?              3. GOSSELIN = EMMA      ROGER      PHILIP   GOSSELIN   RALF
   POMERAI (d. c. 1102)           (d. 1137-41)           │
   │                                                  JOSCELIN
2. WILLIAM = ?
   (d. 1104)
   │
   ETHELWARD      4. HENRY (I) = ROHESIA d. of
                     (d. 1166/7)   KING HENRY I
                     │
5. HENRY (II) = 1. MATILDA DE VITERI
   (c. 1145-94)   2. ROHESIA, d. of THOMAS
                     BARDOLF THE ELDER
   │
6. HENRY (III) = ALICE DE VERNON
   (c. 1170-1207)
   │
                                    WILLIAM      GEOFFREY
7. HENRY (IV) = JOAN d. of ROGER
   (? - 1221)     DE VALLETORT
   │
8. HENRY (V) = MARGARET
   (1211-37?)    DE VERNON
   │
9. HENRY (VI) = ISEULT DE
   (1236?-81)    BATHONIA = WILLIAM DE ALBAMARA
   │
10. HENRY (VII) = AMICIA, d. of GEOFFREY = WILLIAM MARTYN
    (1265-1305)    DE CAUNVILLE
```

172

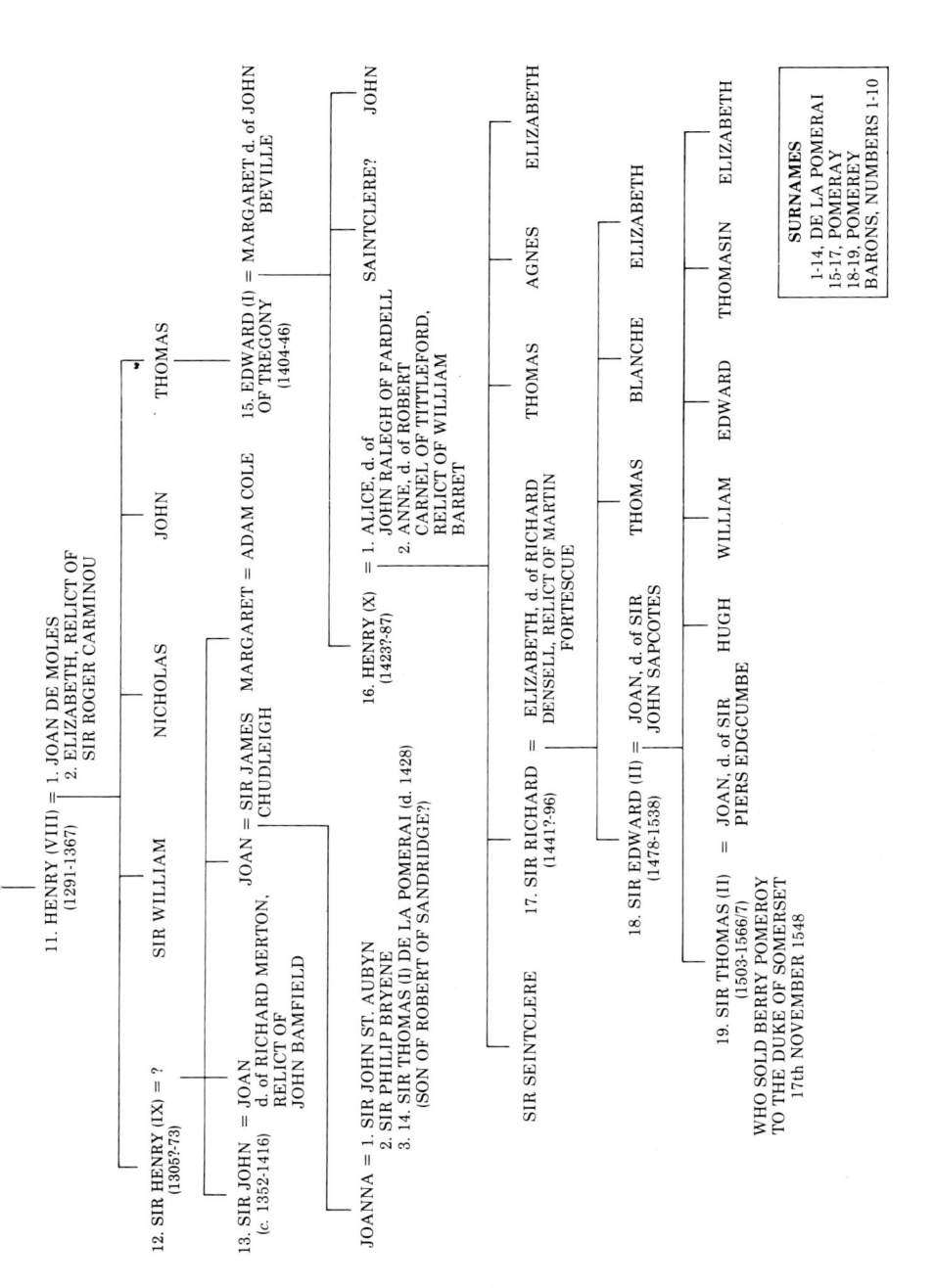

```
                            11. HENRY (VIII) = 1. JOAN DE MOLES
                               (1291-1367)    2. ELIZABETH, RELICT OF
                                              SIR ROGER CARMINOU
          ┌──────────────────────┬─────────────┬──────────┬─────────────────────────────┐
       SIR WILLIAM            NICHOLAS       JOHN      THOMAS              15. EDWARD (I) = MARGARET d. of JOHN
                                                                              OF TREGONY     BEVILLE
                                                                               (1404-46)
   ┌──────────┬──────────────────┬───────────────────────────┐                    │
12. SIR HENRY (IX) = ?      JOAN = SIR JAMES   MARGARET = ADAM COLE    16. HENRY (X) = 1. ALICE, d. of        SAINTCLERE?   JOHN
    (1305?-73)                   CHUDLEIGH                                (1423?-87)     JOHN RALEGH OF FARDELL
                                                                                      2. ANNE, d. of ROBERT
13. SIR JOHN = JOAN                                                                      CARNEL OF TITTLEFORD,
   (c. 1352-1416) d. of RICHARD MERTON,                                                  RELICT OF WILLIAM
                  RELICT OF                                                              BARRET
                  JOHN BAMFIELD
                                                          ┌──────────────────────┬─────────────┬─────────────┐
JOANNA = 1. SIR JOHN ST. AUBYN                      17. SIR RICHARD = ELIZABETH, d. of RICHARD   THOMAS   AGNES   ELIZABETH
         2. SIR PHILIP BRYENE                          (1441?-96)     DENSELL, RELICT OF MARTIN
         3. 14. SIR THOMAS (I) DE LA POMERAI (d. 1428)                FORTESCUE
            (SON OF ROBERT OF SANDRIDGE?)
                                              ┌──────────────┬──────────────────────────────────┐
                                         SIR SEINTCLERE  18. SIR EDWARD (II) = JOAN, d. of SIR        THOMAS    BLANCHE    ELIZABETH
                                                            (1478-1538)        JOHN SAPCOTES
                                                                     │
                                            ┌────────────────────────┼──────────┬──────────┬──────────┬──────────┐
                                  19. SIR THOMAS (II) = JOAN, d. of SIR   HUGH   WILLIAM   EDWARD   THOMASIN   ELIZABETH
                                       (1503-1566/7)    PIERS EDGCUMBE
                                  WHO SOLD BERRY POMEROY
                                  TO THE DUKE OF SOMERSET
                                  17th NOVEMBER 1548
```

SURNAMES
1-14, DE LA POMERAI
15-17, POMERAY
18-19, POMEREY
BARONS, NUMBERS 1-10

King Henry VIII and Jane Seymour

THE SEYMOURS OF BERRY POMEROY

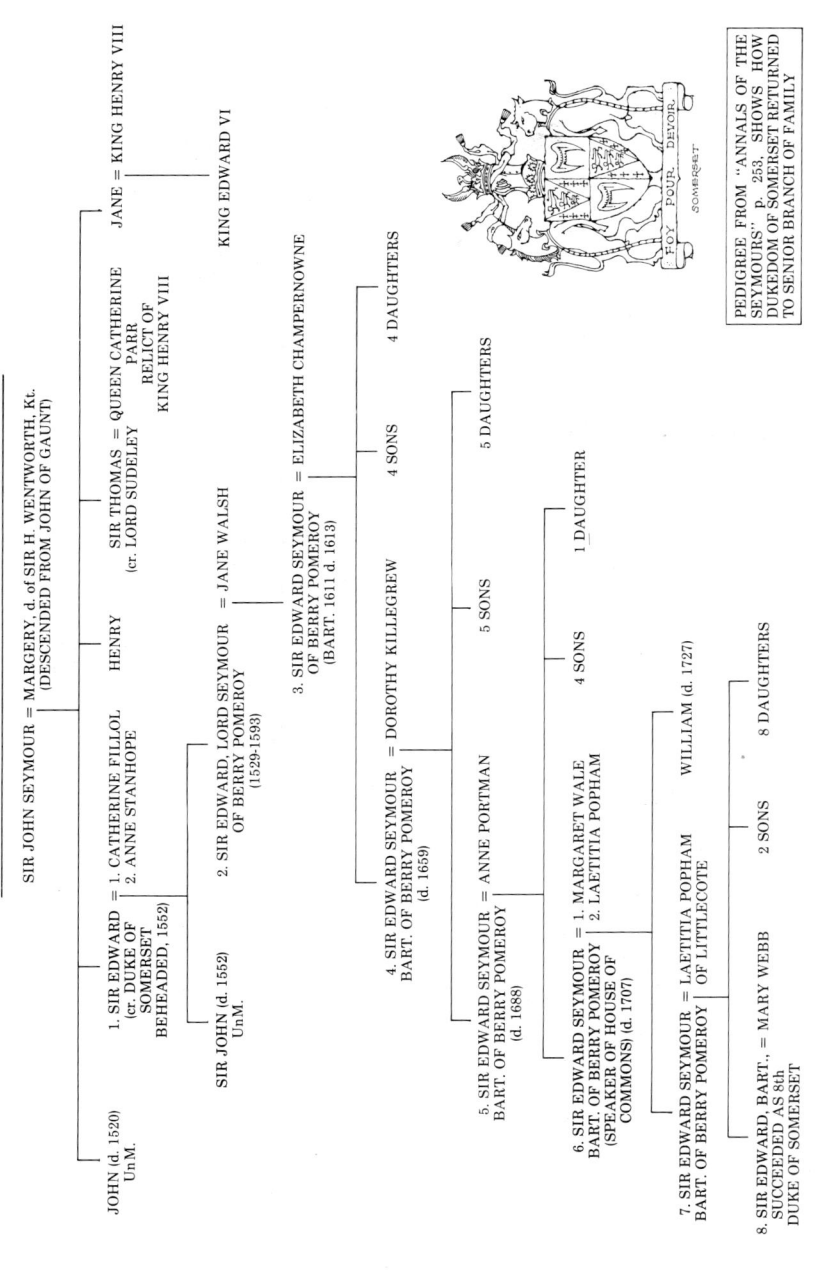

SIR JOHN SEYMOUR = MARGERY, d. of SIR H WENTWORTH, Kt.
(DESCENDED FROM JOHN OF GAUNT)

- 1. SIR EDWARD (cr. DUKE OF SOMERSET BEHEADED, 1552) = 1. CATHERINE FILLOL / 2. ANNE STANHOPE
- HENRY
- SIR THOMAS = QUEEN CATHERINE PARR (cr. LORD SUDELEY) RELICT OF KING HENRY VIII
- JANE = KING HENRY VIII
- KING EDWARD VI

JOHN (d. 1520) UnM.

SIR JOHN (d. 1552) UnM.

2. SIR EDWARD, LORD SEYMOUR OF BERRY POMEROY (1529-1593) = JANE WALSH

3. SIR EDWARD SEYMOUR OF BERRY POMEROY (BART. 1611 d. 1613) = ELIZABETH CHAMPERNOWNE

4 SONS — 4 DAUGHTERS

4. SIR EDWARD SEYMOUR BART. OF BERRY POMEROY (d. 1659) = DOROTHY KILLEGREW

5 SONS — 5 DAUGHTERS

5. SIR EDWARD SEYMOUR BART. OF BERRY POMEROY (d. 1688) = ANNE PORTMAN

4 SONS — 1 DAUGHTER

6. SIR EDWARD SEYMOUR BART. OF BERRY POMEROY (SPEAKER OF HOUSE OF COMMONS) (d. 1707) = 1. MARGARET WALE / 2. LAETITIA POPHAM

WILLIAM (d. 1727) — 2 SONS — 8 DAUGHTERS

7. SIR EDWARD SEYMOUR BART. OF BERRY POMEROY = LAETITIA POPHAM OF LITTLECOTE

8. SIR EDWARD, BART.. SUCCEEDED AS 8th DUKE OF SOMERSET = MARY WEBB

PEDIGREE FROM "ANNALS OF THE SEYMOURS". p. 253. SHOWS HOW DUKEDOM OF SOMERSET RETURNED TO SENIOR BRANCH OF FAMILY

J HAZZARD '81